Writers of Wales

Kate Roberts

Katie Gramich

University of Wales Press

Cardiff 2011

www.uwp.co.uk

British Library Cataloguing-in-Publication Data
A catalogue record for this book is available from the British Library.

ISBN 978-0-7083-2338-0
e-ISBN 978-0-7083-2339-7

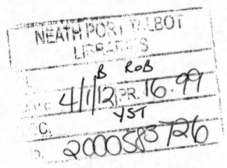

Typeset by Eira Fenn Gaunt, Fenn Typesetting
Printed in Wales by Dinefwr Press, Llandybïe

Writers of Wales

Kate Roberts

Preface

That Kate Roberts (1891–1985) was the most important Welsh female novelist and short story writer of the twentieth century is a fact very few would dispute. She produced a large and various *oeuvre* extending over a period of over half a century. In addition to being a creative writer, she was an influential critic, journalist, editor and publisher, not to mention a political activist and one of the earliest members of Plaid Cymru, the Welsh Nationalist Party – or the BB (Bloody Blaid) as she affectionately referred to it. One might say that she occupies a position in Welsh literature analogous to that enjoyed by Virginia Woolf in English literature, and yet the contrast in the amount and the quality of published critical writings on the two authors' work could hardly be more stark. While the British Library integrated catalogue lists no fewer than 777 items with 'Virginia Woolf' in the title, there are only nineteen items on Kate Roberts, four of which are reprints of the same text by Derec Llwyd Morgan.

This critical introduction to the life and work of Kate Roberts is intended to help remedy the regrettable ignorance of her achievement outside Wales, and to try to begin a contemporary re-engagement with and re-evaluation of her work within Wales.

The author would like to thank the copyright holder for permission to quote from the work of Kate Roberts.

Contents

Illustrations

'Before 1917...': the making of a writer

Born and brought up in the small Caernarfonshire village of Rhosgadfan, the daughter of a formidably capable mother who cared
for the household, children and smallholding, and a hardworking,
stoical quarryman father, Kate Roberts asserted in her 1960 autobiography that 'everything important, everything that made a
deep impression, happened to me before 1917'.[1] What follows,
then, is an examination of this formative background to her life
and work, the cultural and social milieu of Roberts's youth, and
the effect that the First World War had on her life and her self-
fashioning as a writer.

Katherine Roberts was born on 13 February 1891, the eldest of
what would be the four children of Catrin and Owen Roberts.
She also had four older half-siblings, three from her father's first
marriage, and one from her mother's. Her father, a quarryman
and smallholder, was 40 years old at the time of her birth, her
mother thirty-seven. Roberts spent most of her childhood living
in a cottage called Cae'r Gors in the village of Rhosgadfan, today
an arts centre dedicated to the memory of the great writer who
was born and raised within its walls. In the 1890s, it must have
been quite a crowded little dwelling. She had three younger
brothers: Richard, Evan and David, the youngest. Cae'r Gors
means 'the field of the marsh', and the name is an accurate
indication of the landscape surrounding it: this is upland Caernarfonshire, not far from the massive peaks of Snowdonia. The
historian O. M. Edwards, who also had his origins in north-west
Wales, used to assert time and again in his influential lectures
and books of the turn of the twentieth century that 'Wales is a

land of mountains', and that this stubborn geographical fact 'give[s] a unity of character to the people who live among them'.[2] But, as the cultural geographer Estyn Evans has pointed out, no people actually live on these rugged peaks; rather, what gives Wales its distinct 'personality' is the 60 per cent of the country that lies above 500 feet, this great upland mass which is the heartland of Wales and where people like Kate Roberts's family lived, and continue to live. Evans argues that 'the physical continuity of an extensive heartland favoured the survival of old ways and an old language';[3] no one was more conscious of this fact than the adult Kate Roberts. As her autobiography, *Y Lôn Wen* (The White Lane), clearly indicates, she came to see herself, her family and their native community as representative of an old Welsh way of life which was rapidly being eroded. Roberts's life and work, then, can be seen not only as the chronicle of an exceptional individual but as the expression of a representative Welsh sensibility.

The land around Cae'r Gors is indeed marshy, and the biggest natural crops are peat and heather, two products that feature frequently in Kate Roberts's fiction. The landscape also, of course, is rich in another natural material: slate, and the landscape today still bears the scars and traces of the slate quarrying industry which briefly brought prosperity to this bleak and inhospitable but strangely beautiful landscape. These are the uplands, and Kate Roberts is by instinct an upland writer. There are many descriptions in her work of characters climbing to hilltops and looking down on a magnificent and far-reaching view – to the eastern side the ramparts of Snowdonia, and to the west the coastal lowlands of the Llŷn Peninsula, the lovely old town of Caernarfon with its magnificent, if ominous, Norman castle, and the Menai Straits, separating the Welsh mainland from the island of Anglesey (Ynys Môn – Milton's 'Mona'). But when Roberts's characters take their eyes away from the distant prospect, the immediate surroundings are full of small details: the pointed yellow flowers of the gorse, the paler petals of the broom, the fragrant bells of the heather, tumbled granite boulders, outcrops of slate and pools of dark, peaty water.

Kate Roberts was brought up close to the land. She, like her siblings, helped her parents with the smallholding: feeding animals, cleaning their pens, milking cows, gathering heather from the hillsides for fuel, making and carrying hay in order to feed the animals over the long, severe winters. The hard work and constant anxiety of the subsistence farmer's life is continually evoked in Roberts's early fiction. At the same time she brings home to her readers the close intimacy between the smallholders and their animals. It is not surprising to find that in later life the childless Kate Roberts kept a series of dogs as companions, dogs who were clearly of great emotional importance to her and with whom she lived in close proximity. Time and again, particularly in her later stories, characters perceive human qualities in animals, especially dogs, responding to them almost as one would towards a child.

In the 1972 volume entitled *Atgofion* (Memories), based on a radio series of personal memoirs, *Y Llwybrau Gynt* (The Former Paths), Kate Roberts gives an account of her life to date. Tellingly, she begins her talk with an extraordinarily detailed description of the interior of her childhood home, Cae'r Gors. She remembers, it seems, every single tiny detail, from the red tiles of the kitchen floor which she would wash every Saturday to the strange hearthstone made out of an old grave, with the carved words still legible upon it. The volume *Atgofion* contains the reminiscences of four prominent Welsh people from the quarrying area of north-west Wales, three men and Roberts. The three men begin with outdoor scenes: a hill with a magnificent view, a row of houses in Blaenau Ffestiniog, a mad woman wandering the streets of a town, but Roberts begins with an intimate delineation of the domestic space. This is entirely characteristic of her work: most of her stories and novels have domestic settings, and it is in these constrained interior spaces that the dramas of her plots take their course. Like Jane Austen's, Kate Roberts's fictional world tends to be small, domestic and dominated by women. Yet, her memoirs also give an account of her very public adult life: writing and performing drama in the towns of the Tawe valley; in the streets of the Rhondda, canvassing for Plaid Cymru; educating the children of

Ystalyfera and Aberdare; collecting and distributing aid to poor families during the Depression; running a major press and news-paper. And yet at the centre of Roberts's world remains that hearth at Cae'r Gors. The homestead included the adjoining animal sheds; two other parts of the old grave which formed the hearthstone of Cae'r Gors were in the cowshed, propped behind the manger. The writer still remembers the words carved on that gravestone, possibly, she says, the first poetry she ever read, and a particularly macabre englyn it is, as she quotes it in *Atgofion*:

> Gorff a'r galon oeraidd gu – y mae'r gwên
>   A'r gwyneb yn llygru.
> Y mae breichiau wedi brychu,
> Tan garchar y ddaear ddu.
>
> (The dear cold body and heart – the smile
>   And the face are rotting.
> The arms have become mottled,
> Under the prison of the black earth.)

The threat of death was thus graphically present in Roberts's earliest memories, as is also testified in *Y Lôn Wen*, where she remembers vividly the dead body of a quarryman killed in an accident being carried past the house, and the small memorial card for a 12-year-old boy also killed in the quarry. Set against this evidence of a cruel and unremitting outer world is the warmth of the domestic hearth, kept in perfect, shipshape order by the mother, who works hard herself and allots tasks to her offspring. Moreover, the kitchen of Cae'r Gors is the scene not only of work, comfort and sustenance, but also of culture and entertainment – storytelling and singing.

The four small named fields around Cae'r Gors formed part of her childhood world; she speaks of them affectionately and intim-ately, naming them and remembering her childhood game of keeping house on the flat stone in Cae Bach (the little field). Further off, the heather-covered slopes of the mountain, Moel Smythaw, also featured in her known map of the world, since she and her brothers would gather heather there together, an activity remembered with affection and described for example towards the end of her 1936 novel, *Traed mewn Cyffion* (Feet in Chains). More ambivalent is her memory of the centrality of the chapel in the family's life, and yet they spent a large proportion of their time there as children, learning and reciting their Bible verses, attending Sunday school, seiats and literary events. 'Dyna gylch ein bywyd, y tŷ, y capel, y caeau, y ffyrdd, y mynydd', she concludes (That was the circle of our life: the house, the chapel, the fields, the lanes, the mountain).[4] Roberts's recollections of childhood are warm: she recounts humorous incidents, colourful characters, excellent storytellers, naughty cats and funny sayings. Though she never idealizes and characteristically emphasizes economic imperatives, she conjures up a vibrant, stimulating childhood world, despite the restriction of its physical boundaries.

Roberts began to move away from this tight circle of family life in Rhosgadfan when she won a scholarship from Rhostryfan Primary School to the county school in Caernarfon. In line with the educational policies of the time, the education she received here was entirely in English, and she remembers the sense of disorientation she felt as a 13-year-old moving from a virtually monoglot Welsh community to a regime of Englishness. But Welsh was not absent from her experience in Caernarfon for, as she observes in *Atgofion*, although all the teachers were English, all the children were Welsh and spoke Welsh together during breaks and playtimes.

She contracted typhoid within six weeks of starting at the new school and because of her protracted serious illness missed out on most of the excitement of the 1904–5 religious revival which was sweeping the country. She recalls going to hear Lloyd George speak in Caernarfon in 1909 and being reduced to tears by her history teacher who upbraided her for writing an essay condemning Edward I for seeking to unite Wales with England. Yet, as she concedes, she was quite happy during her six years at Caernarfon County School.

In 1910, she went to University College, Bangor, where she was one of a small number of female students in university at that time; she was acutely aware of her privilege and of the financial sacrifice her education meant for her parents. But she blossomed in the college as one of fewer than a hundred female students there altogether; she enjoyed the social life and got to know most of her fellow students at the hostel in Bangor. She studied Welsh under the charismatic John Morris-Jones and the formidable scholar, Ifor Williams, though again, as in the county school, all the lectures were given through the medium of English. The Welsh Society at Bangor was vibrant, and there was much literary and cultural activity: eisteddfodau, debates and student newspapers; the bright, industrious and strikingly good-looking young Kate Roberts was at the heart of this cultural ferment. As she concludes in *Atgofion*, 'dyma amser hapusaf fy mywyd' (this was the happiest time of my life);[5] this is the period before the First World War which she describes as being bathed in 'tegwch y bore' (the fairness of morning) in her 1958 novel of that name. She had a close relationship with fellow-student and poet, David Ellis, during her three years at Bangor; he was later to join the medical corps during the First World War and in June 1918 he disappeared in Salonica. Alan Llwyd and Elwyn Edwards have argued that Roberts later tried to cover up the fact that she and David Ellis had once been lovers, though she did confide it to her friend and co-worker Gwilym R. Jones many years later.[6] Whatever the precise nature of their relationship, the loss of Ellis in the war must have been a source of grief and anger for Kate Roberts at this stage of her life.

But before the advent of the war, Roberts had embarked on a new stage in her life, making use of her expensive education and beginning to repay her parents by becoming a schoolteacher. She left Bangor in 1913 with a second-class honours degree in Welsh and a teacher's certificate. A letter of recommendation from her former lecturer, Ifor Williams, among her papers in the National Library, sheds light on her degree result: he writes on 7 April 1927:

In the University examination Miss Roberts was awarded a Second Class, because she did not attempt the whole paper. There was no doubt as to the first class quality of the work she sent in; but the examiners based their decision on the total aggregate of marks instead of on quality; to my great disappointment our most brilliant student got a second.[7]

Perhaps because she had not gained the First that her lecturers had expected, she took a post as a teacher in Ysgol Elfennol Dol-badarn (a primary school) in Llanberis for a year; her salary here was only £60 a year, and she was unable in the small local school to teach her own specialism, Welsh, leaving her feeling frustrated. She does not describe this period in *Atgofion* but gives it fictional form in her autobiographical novel, *Tegwch y Bore*, where her protagonist, Ann Owen, teaches in the narrow-minded and claus-trophobic community of Blaen-Ddôl before the war. It is the Great War that, ironically, brings Ann employment worthy of her talent and qualifications because she takes over the post of a male teacher who has joined up. This is precisely what happened to Roberts herself in February 1915 when she took up such a teaching post at a secondary school in Ystalyfera in the Swansea valley. The move to 'y Sowth' (the south) was quite a wrench for the home-loving young woman and at first she found it hard to under-stand the unfamiliar dialect. But her memoirs show that she soon overcame that obstacle and began to relish the rich cultural life of the area, as well as teaching at a higher level, and the pleasure of having able pupils in her classes, such as the boy who would later become the great poet, D. Gwenallt Jones. In *Atgofion*, she is warm in her praise of Ystalyfera: 'Yr oedd cymdeithas hapus a phobl hynaws yn y cwm diwylliedig yma' (There was a happy com-munity and friendly people in this cultured valley).[8]

This was the beginning of a twenty-year period of 'exile' in south Wales for Roberts and, although her homesickness for Caer-narfonshire was powerful at times, it is clear that she profited from her different experience there, both as a writer and as a person. Arguably, it was during her time in Ystalyfera that the first inklings of her future life as a writer manifested themselves, for she threw herself enthusiastically into the literary and dramatic activities of the area, as she had done in Bangor as an under-graduate, both co-writing and acting in short plays. She was an active member of Cymdeithas y Ddraig Goch (the Red Dragon Society), which had regular literary meetings and events, re-ported in the local newspaper, *Llais Llafur* (Labour Voice), and she formed a close friendship with two other young women there, Betty Eynon Davies and Margaret Price. These were the two collaborators with her on the plays that the Red Dragon Society performed in the Tawe valley during the war. According to Nia Williams, the three young women were well known locally as 'y tair B.A.' (the three BAs), which indicates the un-usualness in those days and in that place of university-educated women.[9] In addition to Nia Williams's valuable research on this period in Roberts's life, Francesca Rhydderch has written illumin-atingly about this formative period for Roberts as a writer, noting how important collaboration with two female colleagues was for her at the time.[10] Intriguingly, given that Roberts's sub-sequent writing was occasionally criticized for being too un-remittingly sad or humourless, this early work in dramatic form was largely comic. Of course, she and her collaborators were aware that in order to achieve an audience they had to entertain and, perhaps particularly in the sombre time of war, the way to attract an audience was by offering the release and distraction of laughter. Indeed, perhaps the distraction was partly for their own benefit too, since Kate Roberts's own brothers were by now soldiers in the British army, their lives in imminent danger. The intense anxiety of this period is unforgettably rendered in Roberts's retrospective autobiographical novel, *Tegwch y Bore*.

Although the plays that Roberts co-authored and performed during the war were not published until the early 1920s, it is fitting to discuss them in this chapter focusing on the period 'before 1917' – arguably, it was Roberts's experience at collaborative playwriting which first made her believe that she could fashion herself into a writer.

The first play to be formed by the pens of two of 'the three BAs' was *Y Fam* (The Mother), a one-act play subsequently published by the Educational Publishing Co. in London and Cardiff in 1920. Its authors are listed on the title page as Betty Eynon Davies and Kate Roberts, in that order. The play is set in a remote farmhouse in rural Wales the night before Hallowe'en ('nos cyn Calan Gaeaf'). The dramatis personae comprise a father, Ifan and his two wives – the first, Mair and second, Nano – along with his son, Gwyn, his small daughter, Eiry, and an old manservant, Siencyn. The speech in the play is unmistakably that of Roberts's native Caernarfonshire. The play turns on memory, contrasting the loyalty of Siencyn, who lost his beloved, Mary, forty years previously, but still remembers her with intense grief, and his master, Ifan, who was widowed just a year before, and has already taken a second wife. Already, despite the fact that Roberts is still a young woman, the tenor of her work is regretful, looking back at the past and emphasizing the losses and disappointments of life. The situation in the play is both sentimental and melodramatic, reminiscent of late nineteenth-century children's literature and Grimm's fairy tales, where the orphaned children are mistreated by their self-centred, wicked stepmother. In the middle of the night, there is a visitor, Mair, the dead mother, who has come from the 'llan' (the churchyard) because she heard her little daughter, Eiry, crying. The spectral Mair enters the house and comforts both her children, rubbing Gwyn's cold feet to warm them and finally taking Eiry away with her. Ifan and Nano awake suddenly to find Eiry gone: she is discovered lying dead outside, having fallen down the steps. This is very much in the vein of late Victorian child deathbed scenes, both in Welsh and English, as found in the work of Winnie Parry and Moelona, as well as Dickens and Charles Kingsley. The play ends on a strange note, with the repentant Nano thinking that from now on she will never be lonely, since Mair will always be with her. Although the play is far too sentimental for modern tastes, it is interesting from a feminist point of view, since it clearly dramatizes the return of the mother, that figure who, according to French feminist theorists such as Luce Irigaray and Hélène Cixous, has been so thoroughly devalued and expunged from the patri-archal symbolic order. Drawing on fairy tale tropes, Kate Roberts and Betty Eynon Davies create a fictional world in which the mother never in fact dies but constantly haunts the living, particu-larly those young women, like Nano in the play, who seek to escape the responsibility of maternity. The spectre of the mother is inescapable and, while on the surface this is a validation of the traditional, nurturing behaviour of the 'Welsh Mam', there are tensions beneath the surface which are suggestive of the burdens and limitations of the role. Already in this, her earliest, albeit co-authored, published volume, Roberts is beginning to explore the conflicting pulls and pressures within the family, those contra-dictory impulses that make women's lives, particularly, so fraught. At the same time, the play's vigorous language, drawing on the rich dialect of Arfon, foreshadows Roberts's later prose work and is an aspect of the play that can only be attributed to her, since her collaborator was not Welsh speaking. Nevertheless, Betty Eynon Davies was an important influence on her younger collaborator: she had graduated from the University of London in 1905, was widely read and sophisticated in comparison with the girl from Snowdonia, and was already an experienced English-language playwright by the time she came to Ystalyfera in 1913.

Roberts's next published volume is also a co-authored play. *Y Canpunt* (The Hundred Pounds) is subtitled 'a comedy from Cwm Tawe' and is the work of three female playwrights: Margaret Price, Kate Roberts and Betty Eynon Davies, listed in that order on the title page of the play when it was published in a 6d edition by the Welsh Outlook Press in Newtown in 1923. The one-act play has five characters: Mrs Davies, a rich widow; Adelina, her daughter; Jim Davies, her nephew; Mari Myfanwy, Jim Davies's girlfriend; and Sam Price, owner of a coalmine. The play opens, unexpectedly, in English, since Adelina is showing off her command of the language, before she is taken to task unceremoniously by her cousin, Jim, who says 'Siaradwch Gymraeg, ferch!' (Speak Welsh, girl!). The Welsh spoken by the characters is in the dialect of the Swansea valley and is authentic and fluent; although one might suspect that Margaret Price, a native of the area, could take credit for that, it is worth recalling that Kate Roberts had an excellent ear for dialect herself and was able to reproduce south Walian speech convincingly in early stories, such as 'Buddugoliaeth Alaw Jim' (Alaw Jim's Victory). The opening exchange between Jim and his girlfriend, Mari, focuses on dress (a trope that would become central in many of Roberts's later short stories): Jim is afraid that Mari is dressed too 'flightily' to make a good impression on his aunt, from whom he hopes to extract £100 to enable himself and Mari to get married. His aunt owes Jim the £100, which his deceased uncle promised him on his deathbed, but instead of giving him the money, she has a tendency to give him presents: a watch, a satin handkerchief and a picture of Queen Victoria. Mari is contemptuous: 'a lot of old rubbish bought in Woolworth's'. Jim's plan is to invest the money in a new cinema that his friend from Cwmllynfell is about to open. Mari suspects that the aunt might want Jim to marry her daughter, Adelina, but Jim assures her that their sights are on Sam Price, owner of Gors-y-Bryniau colliery, now that he is beginning to make a large profit from it. The name of the colliery is interesting, since it foreshadows the place name in the title of Roberts's first book of short stories, *O Gors y Bryniau* (From the Marsh of the Hills), which would be published two years later. Such a detail offers a glimpse of the collaborative processes of the three women writers: Roberts's north Wales is transposed onto a south Wales landscape.

The play is genuinely funny; Mari is a feisty and admirable heroine, nicely juxtaposed with the snobbish, Anglicized Adelina and her mother. There is a pointed contrast between Mari's lively dialect and the aunt's macaronic, Anglicized Welsh: 'Mae Adelina yn paento yn splendid' (Adelina paints splendidly). Mari manages to extract the £100 from the aunt by flirting outrageously with Sam Price: the aunt finally gives them the £100 in order to get rid of them and clear the path for her daughter to catch the marriageable Mr Price. The play, as its title indicates, and in spite of its broad comedy, turns on economic realities and class differences, and is in that regard reminiscent of the work of the pioneering Anglo-Welsh dramatist, J. O. Francis. Its comic tone and structure, though, ensure that the characters are not ground down by poverty and hardship but triumph over it through their down-to-earth wit.

Before the appearance in print of her next co-authored play, Roberts had already begun to publish work in a different genre, the short story, which she would come to make her own and would be the medium of perhaps her finest literary work. Nevertheless, the experiment with a new genre did not immediately take her away from the stage or from her collaborators. The next play was *Wel! Wel!* (Well, well!), a comedy by Betty Eynon Davies, Margaret Price and Kate Roberts, listed in that order on the title page of the volume published by the Welsh Outlook Press in 1926. It features ten characters: Mrs Gwen Jenkins; her husband Tom; her niece Mair; her mother, Mamgu (Granny); and the customers of their little newsagent/sweet shop in the village of Pentrebach, somewhere in the south Wales valleys. The shop is a locale which will recur many times in Roberts's work, perhaps since it offers a space for women, particularly, to come together outside the confines of the domestic. Analogously, Willy Russell, the contemporary English dramatist best known for his play, *Shirley Valentine*, has attributed his knowledge of the way women interact when men are absent to his experience as a small child, eavesdropping the conversation of female customers in his grandmother's small shop. It is, potentially, a place of shared secrets and revelations, and it is as such that Roberts, like Russell, exploits it.

Mrs Jenkins immediately reveals herself to be a gossip of the first order, and her colourful tales are constantly met by Mamgu's refrain 'Wel! Wel!', a kind of comic catchphrase that would work well in the theatre. Also notable in this play is the racy use of south Welsh dialect. Gossip centres on the comings and goings of Dulyn Jones, the attractive young Nonconformist minister, who is showing all the signs of being about to get married. The customers elaborate a long and, it turns out, completely false story about the minister's being about to marry a widow called Mrs Parry; in fact, the play can be seen as a self-referential one about the way that a story grows and is embellished and consumed. Again, as in *Y Fam*, there are echoes of the fairy or folk tale in this play, as the various customers take on roles to add their pieces of fiction to the growing story, somewhat like the cumulative structure of a traditional tale.

Drawing on a variety of different sources and modes of writing, then, Kate Roberts and her female collaborators produced and acted in three plays during the First World War, which entertained their local community at a time of exceptional anxiety and uncertainty, raised money to send parcels to troops abroad and served as an important apprenticeship for Roberts the budding writer. None of these early, co-authored plays is of enduring literary value but they are significant to a full understanding of how the great writer of fiction, Kate Roberts, began to fashion herself as an author. It is also notable that the protagonists of Roberts's later fictions, Ann in the novel *Tegwch y Bore* (1958) and Bet in the novella *Tywyll Heno* (Dark Tonight; 1962) are both playwrights, writing for the local community. Roberts herself acted in her own co-authored plays and later in life directed performances of *anterliwtiau* (dramatic interludes) by the eighteenth-century playwright, Twm o'r Nant. Moreover, in the 1950s and 1960s, with the advent of new technology, she responded by writing a number of radio dramas and adapting some of her prose works to be broadcast on the BBC. More generally, the discipline of writing vivid dialogue for her dramatic characters undoubtedly helped Roberts in the manipulation of direct speech in her later stories and novels, while the shared experience of crafting a central *agon* or conflict as a pivot for the brief structure of a one-act play must have been useful training for the rigorous structural discipline of the short story genre.

2
From playwright to prose writer: 1917–1928

On 21 November 1918, a short story entitled 'Y Diafol yn 1960' (The Devil in 1960) appeared in the pages of the radical magazine, *Y Darian* (The Shield).[1] It was a coruscating satire of those who initiated, prolonged and profited from a second world war, and its author consigned them all, literally, to eternal damnation. The story is a strange hybrid of science fiction (since it anticipates a possible future) and Christian allegory in the mode of Bunyan or, in the Welsh literary tradition, of the author of *Gweledigaetheu y Bardd Cwsc* (Visions of the Sleeping Bard; 1703), Ellis Wynne. It is also clearly influenced by, and an angry response to, the First World War, which had so recently and painfully come to an end. The story projects a strong voice, a voice of conviction, that of a new writer who most definitely had something to say. It was the voice of Kate Roberts, making itself heard in her first published work of fiction. Over the next sixty years, her literary voice would make itself heard again and again in a lifetime's work of sixteen published volumes of fiction, together with voluminous journalism, criticism, drama and memoir.

'The Devil in 1960' is a striking debut. It is also evidently the work of an inexperienced author writing experimentally, searching for a style to call her own. In subsequent decades, Roberts would eschew the stridency of satire in favour of a much more subtle, understated, even laconic literary voice. Yet, this first venture into fiction is nonetheless suffused with hints and clues that will help lead us to Kate Roberts, the writer, who is, like every writer, and *pace* T. S. Eliot, indivisible from Kate Roberts the woman and suffering human being. 'The Devil in 1960' has a first-person female narrator who is clearly a projection of the author herself, since she speaks of having been a teacher in Y——— and A————, which presumably stand for Ystalyfera and Aberdare. Roberts, the 27-year-old unmarried teacher at Aberdare Girls' County School, imagines a gloomy future for herself forty-two years on, old, alone and 'on the parish' since she has no pension. True to the socialist ethos of the newspaper, the full title of which was *Tarian y Gweithiwr* (The Worker's Shield), she makes a direct reference to the Teachers' Pension Act currently being debated in Parliament – but in this story's dystopian vision, the Act is not passed. On a stormy, snowy night in the future, the narrator receives an unexpected visitor to her comfortless cottage: it is the Devil himself, ousted from hell by the sudden influx of the damned after a second world war. These new inmates are so numerous and so unwilling to accept the Devil's authority that he is forced out of his domain while they continue, in their accustomed fashion, to fight for power. The Devil, meanwhile, plans to establish a new hell in the North Pole, and he solicits the narrator's help to do so. She is just negotiating her terms when she is awoken suddenly from her sleep and finds herself back again in the summer of 1918. It has all been a dream, or rather a sardonic and prophetic nightmare.

The newspaper in which Roberts's first story appeared was an emphatically literary as well as a politically committed publication. It was a weekly which included a short story or a serialised novel in each issue, along with many poems, essays and page after page of Eisteddfod adjudications. Moelona (Elizabeth Mary Jones), probably the best-known Welsh-language female writer of the age, had recently published her novel, *Rhamant y Rhos* (The Romance of the Moor) in its pages. Interestingly, while other contributors habitually use one-word bardic names, such as 'Moelona', 'Debora' and 'Elwyn', Kate Roberts uses her full name for her first published story. It is, as it were, a sign of her earnestness: she does not wish to hide behind any fanciful pseudonym but to stand up and be counted – and recognized – right from the start.

It is fitting that her first published short story should be an impassioned condemnation of war, since she often said in interviews that it was the devastating loss of her younger brother, David (known as Dei), during the war in 1917 that first drove her to write, as a kind of therapeutic activity. She felt at the time that she needed to write or choke with the grief, anger and indignation of the loss. As mentioned above, she used 1917 as a kind of threshold to think about her own life: everything formative had happened to her before that date, and yet the date is, somewhat paradoxically, 'Year One' in the history of Kate Roberts the writer. The story of Dei's death is poignantly recounted in Roberts's autobiography, *Y Lôn Wen*. The suffering was drawn out for Roberts and her family because Dei had been seriously wounded and was recuperating in hospital in Malta, which meant that they were all hoping for months on end for a recovery and a return to Wales (as had already occurred to Roberts's older brother, who had safely returned). Cruelly, though, Dei did not recover and died in hospital in Malta at the age of nineteen. In later life, Roberts made a pilgrimage to the island to visit his grave. It was a loss that overshadowed and shaped her life, as she herself recognized. The writing was – at least at the start – a means of emotional catharsis.

After the publication of that first, angry short story in 1918, Kate Roberts continued to write fiction between that date and the 1925 publication of her first volume of short fiction, *O Gors y Bryniau*. She submitted three stories (all of which would later appear in the volume) to the 1921 National Eisteddfod in Caernarfon but the judge, R. Dewi Williams, placed her work, astonishingly, at the bottom of the second division of submissions and awarded the prize to R. Lloyd Jones. Roberts must have been disappointed but, at the same time, she knew the worth of her own stories and was by no means ready to bow to the opinion of the judge. As she wrote in one of her earliest letters to the poet and dramatist, Saunders Lewis, dated January 1923, 'Nid oeddwn fodlon ar y feirniadaeth ac arhosais hyd amser gwell a beirniad gwell' (I was not happy with the judgement and I (decided to) wait for a better time and better judge).[2]

The three stories were 'Y Chwarel yn Galw'n Ôl' (The Quarry Calling Him Back) (later renamed 'Hiraeth' (Longing)), 'Prentisiaeth Huw' (Huw's Apprenticeship) and 'Y Man Geni' (The Birthmark). 'Y Man Geni' was written in April 1921, while the other two date from May of the same year. All three stories were published in *Cymru* in 1922, while 'Newid Byd' (A Change of World) first appeared in *Yr Efrydydd* (The Scholar) in January 1923. 'Y Llythyr' (The Letter) made its first appearance in print in *Y Llenor* (The Author) in the summer of 1923, and it was *Y Llenor* which also published 'Pryfocio' (Provocation) later the same year, 'Y Wraig Weddw' (The Widow) and 'Henaint' (Old Age) in 1924 and 'Bywyd' (Life) in 1925; the latter was susequently renamed 'Rhigolau Bywyd' (The Ruts of Life), and would become the title of Roberts's second volume of stories.

In the early 1920s, then, Roberts was beginning to establish her reputation both as a popular, community playwright and as a writer of more highbrow short stories, published in a range of the leading Welsh literary magazines. In a letter of 20 January 1923, Saunders Lewis writes to express his admiration of her work, singling out 'Newid Byd' as proof that she is becoming a mistress of the short story genre. In addition to positive reviews and the wholehearted support of a man who would become not only a prominent man of letters and political activist but also the leading critic of the time, interest in translating her stories into other languages was shown from an early stage of her literary career. As early as March 1925, for example, Roberts received a request from Roparz Hemon for permission to translate her story 'Y Wraig Weddw', which had appeared in *Y Llenor* in the previous year, into Breton. In December 1925, L. P. Nemo, the publisher of the Breton journal, *Gwalarn*, wrote to thank Roberts for allowing the translation of her story to appear there, adding 'you cannot imagine how keen people are here on everything that is Welsh . . . Your story has been found very interesting and quite new to us as a psychological study.'[3] Despite rejection by an Eisteddfod judge, then, Kate Roberts must have been encouraged by this enthusiastic interest in her fledgling literary career. At any rate, she wasted no time in collecting together the stories that she had published in magazines and brought out her first volume of fiction in 1925.

O Gors y Bryniau was published by the Wrexham firm of Hughes and Son and contains nine short stories, written between 1921 and 1924. Kate Roberts's first published volume is rooted in a particular place, as the title itself immediately announces. Her family home, Cae'r Gors, in Rhosgadfan, Caernarfonshire, is hinted at in the title, while the landscape evoked in most of the stories is very specifically the upland landscape of her childhood. The title suggests that these stories come from the marshland in the hills, just as the author herself does, and the characters and events of the stories are very much shaped by the place. The community evoked in the stories is the close-knit, Welsh-speaking community of smallholders and quarry workers in which Roberts herself was raised, and the temporal setting is generally in the early years of the twentieth century, some stories being specifically dated as being set during the First World War.

The stories are all concerned with *hiraeth* (longing) in one form or another, one of the central stories having that word as its title. In this sense, the volume is redolent of the grief-stricken atmosphere of post-First World War Wales. In addition to Kate Roberts's un-assuageable grief at the death of her youngest brother in the war, there is also a strong feeling of displacement from the native place, a homesickness and a longing for return which must derive at least partly from Kate Roberts's own situation. From the middle of the war, as we have seen, she had been living in what her characters call 'y Sowth', first as a teacher in Ystalyfera, and latterly at Aberdare Girls' Grammar School. Time and again in the stories, her characters long to return, even when they are dimly aware that such a return – particularly to work in the slate quarries – is a mortal threat. Indeed, if *hiraeth* is the dominant emotional tone of the volume, the central locus is the slate quarry itself, which forms a kind of un-narrated black hole (a 'twll du', as it is called in the stories) to which Roberts's male characters are, often fatally and yet ineluctably, attracted.

The first story, 'Y Man Geni', focuses on Tomos, who is a scholarship boy at the county school but is not thriving there because he is afflicted by guilt at the thought of the financial sacrifice his widowed mother is making for his education. He is drawn to the slate quarry, where his father was killed, and where his father's older brother also perished. All three are called Tomos and have a birthmark on their face. The focus in this story on poverty and hardship in the slate-quarrying community of Caernarfonshire is entirely characteristic of Roberts's early prose work. What is unusual in this very early story is the use of the symbolic birthmark, a mark which, like the Biblical mark of Cain, appears to doom the menfolk of Arfon to repeating the same life pattern, leading inevitably to suffering and death. The story is quietly written, poignant in its simplicity, resonant in its inwardness, for the consciousness of the story is centred on the tormented thoughts and memories of the boy, Tomos. The story, though, is sad, not only because of the accidental death of the boy at its end – he falls into the quarry – but because there is a suggestion of determinism: there is no escape from this repeated cycle of suffering and sacrifice. This determinism is already suggested by the double meaning of the story's title in Welsh: 'man geni' can mean both birthmark and place of birth. It is as if being born in this particular place is itself a kind of curse, condemning the inhabitants to lives of pain and loss. The story is reminiscent of J. M. Synge's *Riders to the Sea* (1904) in its stark representation of the inexorability of death for the poor worker and the pietà-like vision of the mourning mother.

The next story shifts the focus squarely onto the mother, rather than the son. 'Prentisiaeth Huw' opens with a focus on Ann Jôs, quarryman's wife, doing the washing. The scene is one that will be repeated many times in Roberts's *oeuvre*: a woman carrying out the hard, physical labour which was involved in domestic work before the advent of household machines. This common task for working-class women is exacerbated for Roberts's character by the challenge of trying to extract the filth of the quarry from the workman's clothing. This tells a similar story to 'Y Man Geni' in the sense that the son, Huw, returns from town where he is an apprentice in a draper's shop to work in the quarry with his father. The whole tenor of this story is more positive, albeit open-ended. Like many south Welsh coal-mining narratives of the 1930s, the story reflects the mother's desire for her son to escape from the clutches of the black hole in the ground to the safer haven of work in a shop, but the boy seems determined, in more senses than one, to end up in that place of dirt and doom which actively, perhaps malevolently, 'calls him back'.

'Hiraeth' actually shifts the setting to that other 'black hole', the coal mine in south Wales. Here, John Robaits, collier, becomes homesick for the north when he receives a letter from his old workmate in the quarry, William. John is then injured in the pit. Even at this very early stage of her career, Roberts renders the dialect of the south with accuracy in the speech of Morgan Hopcyn, John's fellow worker, who comes to break the news. Hopcyn is also depicted positively, as a gentle and compassionate man. John has to have his leg amputated and the family returns to the north at the end. Ironically, Elin Robaits, who had been set against returning to the north, is the one who is forced to write to ask for an easy job for her husband in the old quarry. Again, the pattern of inevitable return to the quarry is repeated, as well as that of injury or death constantly threatening the industrial worker.

'Yr Athronydd' (The Philosopher; dated March 1922) is a rather different story stylistically. It focuses on an eccentric old bachelor who stays at home reading all day after an accident in the quarry years before disabled him. His sister's infant daughter, Luned, has just died, and he is suddenly drawn out of his self-absorption. His sister, Meri, has also lost her oldest son in the war; Ifan begins to question why such apparently senseless deaths happen. Still pondering and questioning the existence of a God, he walks into the mountains and the story enters into the realms of fantasy. Ifan hears music and sees two beautiful dancers; at the same time, Roberts's habitually spare, realist prose becomes unusually figurative and poetic. In describing the girl whom Ifan sees dancing on the mountain, Roberts describes her thus: 'Yr oedd llygaid y ferch cyn ddued â chysgod Castell y Dre ar Afon Menai noson ddigynnwrf yn yr haf' (The girl's eyes were as black as the shadow of the Town Castle on the river Menai on a still summer's evening), while her male partner has 'wallt o wineu gwan yr hydref a'i lygaid o liw môr ar ôl storm' (hair the colour of the light auburn of Autumn and eyes the colour of the sea after a storm).[4] The beautiful young couple explain that they are from the family of Lleu and Llŷr, that they have been expecting him for a long time and that they live on the fruits of the mountain. No one dies among them. Ifan takes the opportunity to ask them if they have poetry but they respond that they have no need of it: poetry can only exist where there is fear and death. Ifan sees Luned among the children playing around them and he goes to her and embraces her; they enter a cave together and disappear, a scene reminiscent of the end of Browning's 'Pied Piper of Hamelin'. What is striking about this fantastical story is its refusal of any Christian afterlife in favour of a distinctly Celtic Otherworld. The story is rooted in the harsh economic and physical realities of the quarrying area of Arfon, but it moves effortlessly into a magic realm situated at the heart of Snowdonia, and derived from the magical medieval prose tales of the *Mabinogion*, which Roberts would have studied at university, taught in school, and which remained a constant inspiration for her own writing.

'Newid Byd' (A Change of World; dated October 1922) is a story singled out by Saunders Lewis for praise and as an example, he says, of the way in which Roberts's stories are moving away from any temptation to moralize. The central character is Wiliam Gruffydd, a quarryman who retired three years before and moved from his smallholding to a house ironically named 'Bodlondeb' (contentment) since Wiliam is far from content and yearns to be back at work in the quarry. The quarry is described as 'Jerusalem ei fyd' (the Jerusalem of his world).[5] On a sudden impulse, he decides to return to the quarry one day; unfortunately, his reception is not what he had hoped for – his old workmates are embarrassed and tongue-tied and his place in the cabin has been taken by loud-mouth show-off, Morgan Owan. Wiliam is dismayed. They discuss 'spitsh y Mawr' (the Big Man's speech), which Wiliam thinks nothing of, since in his view it shows that the Big Man has turned his back on the *gwerin*, the common people. Morgan Owan volubly disagrees. Wiliam argues that Y Mawr shows his disregard for the workers by being all too ready to send their sons to war (it is indicated that the war is still going on), 'achos plant y gweithiwrs ceith hi gleta ymhob Rhyfal' (because it's the workers' children who get the worst of it in every war).[6] Roberts takes delight in mocking Morgan, the ardent supporter of Y Mawr, who is clearly meant to be Lloyd George, by placing ridiculously pretentious and meaningless words in his mouth. It is strongly suggested that the 'fog' of words used by Morgan and his hero blind many of the workers. Writing in the early 1920s, a time when Lloyd George was viewed as the apostle of peace at Geneva, Kate Roberts here reveals a palpable political agenda. She is calling attention to the bankruptcy of Liberalism and its claim to speak for the interests of the *gwerin* of Wales. After all, 1925, when *O Gors y Bryniau* was published, was also the year in which Plaid Genedlaethol Cymru (The National Party of Wales, later Plaid Cymru) was founded, partly in reaction to the disillusionment of Welsh nationalists with Lloyd George, the failed Home Rule movement and, over-whelmingly, with the First World War. It is no wonder, then, that Saunders Lewis singled out this story for special praise, for it seems to speak of the two writers' shared political commitment to the fledgling nationalist party. At the same time, this story is one of the very rare instances in which Kate Roberts would ever come near to writing in an overtly political way in her creative work. What is remarkable is that she managed to separate her strongly held political views from her creative writing, which never descends into propaganda. Even in 'Newid Byd', the political satire is sketched in as a background to the story's centre of interest, which remains on the feelings the old man, making the story in the end a poignant meditation on old age and loneliness, rather than a polit-ical squib.

Just as 'Newid Byd' is set during the First World War, the next story, 'Y Llythyr' (The Letter; dated March 1923) is also a wartime story, and is one of the few to be precisely dated: in November 1917. Wmffra is the central character, and he is away from home, working on the railway in Liverpool and feeling homesick for Caernarfonshire (as Kate Roberts's own father was forced to do during the war). The whole of the first half of the story consists of Wmffra's self-sustaining memories of a perfect Saturday at home when he took his greyhounds and ferrets out hunting. His two fellow workers urge him to write a letter to Ann, his wife, but he never does. They don't suspect that Wmffra is actually illiterate, having played truant consistently rather than attend school in his childhood. But he finally succumbs to his friends' urging; the scene then cleverly switches, in a cinematic way, to focus on Ann receiving the letter. At first she is convinced that it is bad news about her husband but then she opens it and finds that he has simply drawn a picture of a greyhound with a rabbit in its mouth. The picture speaks volumes of his longing for home and, tellingly, as soon as the youngest child, Robin, sees it, he immediately associates it with his 'tada' (daddy). Although this story turns upon familiar themes of homesickness and economic pressures, the story is relatively light-hearted, reflecting perhaps the simple pleasures and delight of Wmffra and his dogs. It is also a story that shows the author's deep empathy with those people of her own background without the educational advantages which took Roberts herself out of that precarious existence.

These stories move democratically to and fore between the genders, now focusing on women's experiences, now on men's. 'Pryfocio' actually begins with two women discussing men: Meri is dismissive of men's selfishness while Catrin is more willing to concede that some men may be different. The focus shifts to their respective marriages, both of which turn out to be less than ideal. Catrin's husband, Wil, is lazy and takes delight in provoking her. Meri advises her to provoke him back. Mention is made of domestic violence, which Catrin's neighbour suffers at the hands of her husband, though Wil is apparently too lazy to lift a finger even to beat her. Catrin is not consoled by Meri's general attack on men: 'yn ei thyb hi ei hunan, hi oedd yr unig ferthyr o wraig yn yr ardal. Ac y mae cael y fraint o fod yr unig ferthyr mewn ardal yn galondid i ddosbarth neilltuol o bobl. Felly Catrin Owen' (in her own opinion, she was the only martyred wife in the neighbourhood. And to have the privilege of being the only martyr in a neighbourhood is a great comfort to a particular type of person. Catrin Owen was such a person).[7] But she reaches the end of her tether when she returns to her house to find that Wil has chopped up their only bed and used it for firewood. She announces her intention to go and drown herself; Wil promptly recommends the best lake nearby for the purpose. The tone of the narrative is quite mixed: potentially tragic feelings and events are treated in a humorous, farcical manner: 'Dyma'r llyn [Llyn yr Hafod] yr âi pawb yn yr ardal iddo i roddi pen ar eu heinioes, pan fyddent wedi blino byw' (This was the lake [Hafod Lake] that people in the neighbourhood went to in order to do away with themselves, when they had got tired of living).[8] Her husband of thirty years urges her on to throw herself in but she turns on her heel and goes home. The ending is somewhat anticlimactic but the story certainly presents a negative portrait of marriage as a kind of continual torment for the wife. The story also shows Roberts's abiding fascination with gender roles and conflicts; while she does not hesitate to represent the shortcomings of men, neither does she portray women in an altogether positive light. In a move that would become characteristic of her short stories, she touches on those places which are tender, controversial and often taboo, such as the masochism of some oppressed women. It is clear even from this early, farcical story that she is not content to be a straightforwardly feminist writer, attacking patriarchy and championing women, despite the centrality of female experience in much of her work.

'Y Wraig Weddw' is an example of this central focus on women's feelings and experiences; the widow of the title is Dora Lloyd, who has lost her husband five years previously. At the start of the story we see her in a typical self-searching mode of women's fiction, standing in front of the mirror, contemplating herself. Her clothing is coded, recording precisely the number of years that have passed since her widowhood: the year before, her silk blouse had black stripes and was done up to the top; this year the blouse is white and she leaves the top buttons undone. This detail is indicative of the care and precision with which Roberts always describes women's clothing: it invariably constitutes a sartorial code, indicative of the woman's personality, status or desires. Like so many of the male characters in these stories, Ned, her husband, was killed in the quarry; the pain of his loss is now beginning to diminish and grow more distant. She is reluctantly preparing to go and visit her sister-in-law on a holiday (Whitsun) when they traditionally reminisce about Ned but she is now thinking of Bob Ifans, himself a widower, who has made her fall half in love with him on account of his kindness to her. She decides to wear a blue skirt, rather than the black, in order to prepare her sister-in-law to learn about her developing relationship with Bob Ifans.

However, on her way out Dora learns from a neighbour that Bob has not even placed a gravestone on his first wife's grave and suddenly Dora knows that she can have nothing more to do with him. This realization is rendered dramatically as: '"Clic" ebe rhywbeth . . . yn ei chalon, fel drws yn cau ac yn cloi ohono'i hun. A gwyddai Dora Lloyd y foment honno, fod Bob Ifans y tu allan i'r drws hwnnw' (Something went 'click' in her heart, like a door shutting and locking of its own accord. And Dora knew from that moment on, that Bob Ifans was outside the door).[9] She immediately returns to her house and changes from her blue skirt into the black one before going on to visit her sister-in-law. Another consequence of shutting Bob out of her heart is that she determines to have the calf back from where she had sent it to graze on better pastures; the description of the calf and her quasi-maternal delight in it makes it clear that it is a child substitute and connected with her dead husband. She will have the calf back to take the place of Bob Ifans in her heart. And yet when the treasured calf returns, the creature ignores her; she thus associates him with the heartless Bob. In the end, we see her milking her cows and singing 'Mae gennyf cwpwr cornel,/A'i lond o lestri te . . .' (I've got a corner cupboard/ With a china tea set inside . . .), as if she has resigned herself to what she has already in her house, rather than searching for another being to lavish her affection upon.[10] The story acts as a counterpoint to 'Pryfocio', showing that independence is, in the end, despite the promptings of desire, probably more advantageous than marriage for women. Both of these stories are also slightly reminiscent in tone of the early dramas: there is a farcical, almost comical element hovering around their edges, despite the fundamental bleakness of the subjects.

'Henaint', the final story in the volume, is arguably both the bleakest of them all and the most haunting. At its centre is a senile old woman who bears comparison with a number of other older women in later stories, such as 'Nain' (Grandma) in the 1930 volume, *Laura Jones*. Clearly, Roberts is interested in what happens to one's identity in extreme old age, and explores here whether loss of memory can actually mean a kind of release from the burdens of responsibility, duty and maternal care. The first-person speaker of this story, though, is an unnamed 44-year-old man who, though he claims not to be one for harping much on the past, has been prompted to let his memory go back thirty-two years to recall his schooldays and his friendship with Twm Llain Wen. The memories that return to him are highly immediate and sensuous, reminiscent of those that Roberts herself would recall of her own schooldays in her autobiographical work, *Y Lôn Wen*, some forty years later. It is interesting, for instance, that the narrator should remember the touch of his teacher's velvet bodice on his cheek as she bent over to mark his sums. This gentle, quasi-maternal gesture contrasts sharply with the devastating loss of all maternal feeling that the ensuing story narrates. Twm Llain Wen, a quarryman, has recently died, and the narrator laments his friend's passing, remembering his passion for choral singing and his zest for life. Twm's mother is now eighty-eight and all she remembers is her own youth; though Twm had been the apple of her eye, she has no recollection of him now and, therefore, can feel no pain at his illness and early death. There is a very detailed description of the old woman's antiquated clothes, which have remained the same throughout her long life, ironically enough, since the woman inside them has changed out of all recognition. The last words of the story are those of the old woman who, on being told that her son Twm has died, replies that she does not know who Twm is. The story ends, dramatically and poignantly, at that point. 'Henaint' connects back to the opening story of the volume, 'Y Man Geni,' not only in suggesting the span of human life (from birth to extreme old age) but also in returning to offer a different perspective on that strongest of bonds, the mother–son relationship. In this final story, even that human bond is slipped, leaving a despairing feeling of human loneliness and futility.

Every single one of these early stories mentions the slate quarry, many of them centring upon it as the source of both life and death. Every story also places emphasis on work, particularly women's hard domestic labour, and on familial relationships. The centre of consciousness varies from story to story, as if deliberately building up a picture of a whole community, including fathers, mothers, children, bachelors, widows, quarrymen, small farmers and shop workers. Notable by their absence are Nonconformist ministers. Although the chapel is mentioned, it features as a social and cultural centre for the community; for Roberts's characters, gossip and literature are much more important than theology. This is in marked contrast to the representation of rural west Wales given in Caradoc Evans's notorious volume of short stories, *My People*, published just ten years previously, which shows the Welsh as oppressed and held in poverty and ignorance by their self-serving, hypocritical Nonconformist pastors.

Kate Roberts's first volume is thus intensely personal: geographically, culturally and temporally specific; and yet speaks not only of a common early twentieth-century feeling of deracination and displacement but also of human bonds and conflicts, the longing for what is lost, and the desire for the unattainable. Far from being trivial or about 'unimportant' domestic matters, this fiction unerringly addresses the most intense human experiences, often the most resistant to articulation. If Roberts sought catharsis from her own bereavement and loneliness in writing these stories, she succeeded in speaking with a voice that transcends the personal and the minority language of which she was, from the outset, an acknowledged mistress.

In the 1920s, then, Kate Roberts was an ambitious and intensely self-critical new author. She was reading widely and searching for models for her own writing, not only within the Welsh literary tradition but much further afield. Early on in her lengthy correspondence with Saunders Lewis, for instance, she expresses her admiration for Katherine Mansfield: 'Y hi yn anad neb a wnaeth imi deimlo nad oes gennyf y syniad lleiaf beth yw stori fer' (She more than anyone made me feel that I hadn't the faintest idea what a short story was).[11] A few years later she wrote to Lewis expressing her continuing dissatisfaction with her own work and saying that when she reads and rereads Chekhov she blushes to think that she had been so bold as to publish a book that called itself a volume of short stories. She is particularly annoyed with herself for spoiling the excellent material she had in 'Henaint', since she thinks the technique of the story is terrible.[12] She also notes as an influence the Irish short story writer, Jane Barlow, whose volume *By Beach and Bogland* (1905) showed her that something could be done with the short story form in Wales.[13] These comments show that, in addition to her thorough immersion in Welsh literature, Roberts went far beyond Wales to look for literary models for her work and that she was particularly interested in the work of other female authors.

The correspondence between Lewis and Roberts in this period also shows that he lent her James Joyce's *Portrait of the Artist as a Young Man*, observing that Joyce had influenced both Morris T. Williams (her future husband) and the poet and editor, E. Prosser Rhys. Roberts admired Joyce's novel a great deal; she expressed her appreciation to Lewis thus: 'dyna athrylith Joyce. Mae yna ryw allu, rhyw bŵer ofnadwy sydd yn torri fel cyllell injan ladd gwair a chwyrnella'r gwair i'r awyr am funud, ond a edy ar ei ôl, res dwt, wastad o wair. Meddylier am bregeth yr offeiriad hwnnw ar uffern gan Joyce' (that is Joyce's genius. There's this ability, this awful power which cuts like the blade of a mower that blows the hay into the air for a minute but which leaves behind a neat, sleek row of hay. Think of that clergyman's sermon about hell by Joyce).[14] Indeed, perhaps Kate Roberts herself was thinking of Joyce when she wrote the powerful passage in her next published volume, *Deian a Loli* (1927), where the obnoxious 'sgŵl' (school-master) puts the fear of hell into the child protagonists: '"Wyddoch chi i le bydd plant fel chi yn mynd ar ôl marw? . . . Mae'r Rhodd Mam newydd yn dweud mai lle o boen i gosbi pechod ydyw uffern," âi ymlaen, "ond roedd yr hen Rodd Mam yn dweud mai llyn yn llosgi o dân a brwmstan oedd o, a'r hen Rodd Mam sy'n iawn," meddai' (Do you know where children like you go when you die? . . . The new catechism says that hell is a place of pain where sin is punished – he went on – but the old catechism said that it's a burning lake of fire and brimstone, and it's the old catechism that's right).[15] He then punishes them by caning, bringing the stick down on their hands 'fel nerth cwymp mewn chwarel' (with the force of a fall of rocks in the quarry).[16] In this way we see Roberts writing in an analogous way to some notable Modernist contemporaries, such as Joyce, but stamping her own vision and culture indelibly upon her writing.

Despite the fact that many of Roberts's early stories are set in her native north-west Wales, it is nevertheless indisputable that she began her career as a writer while she was living in the south. We have already seen how the vibrant and cultured society of Ystalyfera fostered her interest in the theatre and encouraged her to experiment with playwriting. By the end of 1917 she had moved to Aberdare, to a post in the girls' county school there, and it was while living in Aberdare that she learned of her young-est brother's death, and that of her close college friend, David Ellis. These bereavements were to have a decisive effect on her life and on her development as a writer, as previously discussed. Mihangel Morgan, in an acerbic essay on Roberts's sojourn in his native Aberdare, notes that although she refers to the town as hell in her letters to Saunders Lewis, when she arrived towards the end of the First World War she had published virtually nothing, but by the time she left in 1928 she was already an established author with a growing reputation.[17] Morgan argues that it was in fact the much-maligned Aberdare and the people she met there who made her into a writer, just as much as the loss of her brother, to which she herself attributed the beginning of her literary career.

Just as she had thrown herself into community activities in Ystalyfera, she did likewise in Aberdare, becoming a prominent member of the Cymmrodorion Society, rising to vice-president and then president by 1925. Yet, her energetic community activity was soon to be channelled in a different, more political, direction. Plaid Genedlaethol Cymru was founded in 1925 and at first Kate Roberts, an instinctive socialist, was reluctant to join, but by 1926 she had not only become a member but found herself landed with the role of chair of the women's committee. Joining the party signalled a decisive step in Roberts's life as a political campaigner and journal-ist, but it also had directly personal consequences, for it was in the first Plaid summer school in Machynlleth in 1926 that she met the man who would become her husband, Morris T. Williams.

While Roberts began to write regularly at this time for Plaid's official journal, *Y Ddraig Goch* (The Red Dragon), she was also preparing her second volume of short stories for the press. *Deian a Loli* (*Deian and Loli*; 1927) is dedicated to the memory of 'Fy mrawd Dafydd a fu farw yn y Rhyfel Mawr yn bedair ar bymtheg oed' (My brother David who died in the Great War at the age of nineteen). The stories were first published serially in *Y Winllan* (The Vineyard), a Wesleyan magazine for children, edited by E. Tegla Davies, in early 1923. As John Emyr, editor of the 1992 reissue of the volume observes, 'Yn ddiweddarach – yn *Traed mewn Cyffion*, yn arbennig – y byddai'r awdures yn mynd i'r afael a hanes colli David. Yn *Deian a Loli*, fel yn *Laura Jones* a *Te yn y Grug*, darlunnir yr amser hapus cyn y dyddiau du' (Later – particularly in *Feet in Chains* – the author would grapple with the story of David's loss. But in *Deian and Loli*, as in *Laura Jones* and *Tea in the Heather*, the happy times before the darkest days are represented).[18] Certainly the characters Deian and Loli in the volume of that name can be seen as childhood versions of Kate Roberts and her youngest brother, David, and these stories can thus be viewed as nostalgic tributes to their shared childhood. They bear comparison with George Eliot's 'Brother and Sister' sonnets, celebrating the innocent and close bond between siblings before they are torn apart. The stories themselves are uneven in tone – occasionally, the voice of the schoolmistress, which Roberts was at the time of their composition, becomes too didactic and even patronizing. She sometimes explains the meaning of words to her supposed juvenile audience, and also provides a glossary. And yet the stories do not shy away from painful or unpleasant experiences.

The setting for the stories is virtually identical to most of the stories in *O Gors y Bryniau*: the twin children live in a small-holding called Bwlch y Gwynt (The Wind's Gap) on the slopes of Moel y Grug (Heather Mountain), and their father works in the slate quarry, while their mother rules the home. The family of Elin and Elis Jôs, and their children Magi, Twm, Wil, Deian and Loli, is not dissimilar to the family we find in the later novel, *Feet in Chains*. Much attention is given to the mother's domestic work and there are a number of anecdotes that sound as if they are humorous family tales, as well as certain turns of phrase, which seem to have been saved from memories of childhood, such as: 'Dywedai Elin Jôs bob amser am ei thŷ pan fyddai yno lanast, megis llanast diwrnod golchi: "Mae'r tŷ yma fel tŷ Jeroboam, bobol." A phan fyddai yno lanast anghyffredin o fawr, dywedai: "Mae'r tŷ yma fel tŷ Jeroboam mab Nebat"' ('Elin Jones would always say of her house when it was in a mess, such as the mess of washing day: "This house is like the house of Jeroboam, folks." And when there was a particularly bad mess, she would say: "This house is like the house of Jeroboam son of Nebat"').[19]

The fact that Deian and Loli are twins allows Roberts to explore gender differences in a subtle way. When the two first attend school at the age of four, they are themselves unable to distinguish between the two of them, so that when asked their names, they reply in unison 'Deian a Loli'. However, as time passes, the way in which they are treated and the gender expectations placed upon them forces them apart. Deian is drawn to mathematics, Loli to stories and playing house. Perhaps the most striking passage in the book is the essay that Loli writes on the topic of 'The Cat' set by the teacher: instead of defining and describing the creature in the Gradgrindian way expected, Loli instead writes an essay in the first-person, as if she were a cat, creating a funny and endearing narrative. But the teacher is unimpressed, much to Loli's indignation. Roberts, herself of course a teacher, has Loli conclude that 'teachers know nothing about these things'.[20] By the end of the volume, Deian has won a scholarship to the county school, having vowed never to go to the quarry like his father, but Loli has failed the exam and is destined – like so many thousands of Welsh girls at that time – to go into domestic service in London. Loli realizes that they will no longer be able to call themselves 'Deian a Loli' in the same breath from now on; it is a sad ending, an echo perhaps of the grief felt by its author at the parting from her own brother, lost during the war.

Saunders Lewis wrote to Roberts in October 1923, saying that he had enjoyed reading *Deian a Loli* and urging her to publish the stories. Yet, he also advises her not to write more stories for children, since he does not consider it to be her true milieu. He recommends that she reads the stories of Katherine Mansfield, a piece of advice that, as we have seen, Roberts would take and from which she would profit.[21] Lewis was clearly concerned that Roberts should not follow in the footsteps of talented but limited Welsh women writers such as Winnie Parry (author of the juvenile novel, *Sioned*) and Fanny Williams (author of another children's novel, *Cit*) and should instead emulate the more ambitious and challenging Modernist path of Mansfield, who wrote of, but not for, children. Many years later, in reviewing Roberts's 1964 collection, *Hyn o Fyd* (A World Such as This), Saunders Lewis would write that there was 'a streak of sentimentality . . . in those early short stories . . . for children' but, he added, using an image suggestive of the drowning of kittens, 'she smothered that'.

That Saunders Lewis's advice to move away from writing for children was sound is suggested by the less than adequate reception of *Deian a Loli*: Ifan ab Owen Edwards in his review of it in *Cymru*, refers to it as a 'llyfr bach deniadol a swynol' (an attractive and charming little book) while Gwenda Gruffydd in *Y Llenor* uses the same adjective, 'swynol' (charming) to describe the stories. As Eigra Lewis Roberts remarks, it is hard to see how anyone who has read the stories would think this an appropriate description of them.[22] But this was typical of the unintentionally patronizing reception of writing for children in the period; neither Lewis nor Roberts herself would have been happy with such anodyne critical judgements.

The full official name of Loli in *Deian a Loli* is Laura Jones, and this is the title of the 1930 volume which can be seen as a sequel to the earlier book of stories. Though generally well received, *Laura Jones* was given an unfavourable review by Iorwerth C. Peate in *Y Llenor*; Roberts was understandably angry but a letter to Saunders Lewis shows that she was able to laugh at the reviewer: 'Y jôc fawr yn y tŷ hwn er neithiwr ydyw bod Peate, Peate o bawb, yn sôn am ddiffyg synnwyr digrifwch. Mae'r peth yn ddigon i wneud i gathod chwerthin' (The big joke in this house since last night is that Peate, Peate of all people, should complain that it lacks a sense of humour. The thing's enough to make a cat laugh).[23] The mention of 'yn y tŷ hwn' (in this house) is suggestive of Roberts's new domestic situation as wife to Morris T. Williams, whom she had married two days before Christmas in 1928. Williams may have made it possible for the famously thin-skinned Kate Roberts to laugh off the negative review in a way she might not have been able to do alone. Certainly, the phrase 'yn y tŷ hwn' suggests a place of unity and solidarity, a place whose inhabitants are in accord, able to laugh together against the world.

Indeed, perhaps that defiant attitude had been necessary in entering into the marriage in the first place. Roberts was nearing forty at the time, while Morris T. Williams was ten years her junior. None of her family was present at the wedding and much of the extant correspondence of that time consists of friends and acquaintances sending belated congratulations on a marriage about which they can barely conceal their astonishment. Siân Williams (wife of Kate Roberts's close friend and fellow short-story writer, D. J. Williams), for instance, sends Roberts a congratulatory letter of characteristic warmth but she seems not even to know the name of her friend's new husband.[24] In the extensive collection of personal photographs in the Kate Roberts archive in the National Library of Wales, there is not a single wedding photograph. Although Roberts and Morris T. Williams had been courting for more than two years at the time, correspondence between them shows that both had qualms about marriage, and the circumstances of the wedding suggest that the couple threw caution to the winds and got married, giving hardly anyone else any forewarning. Correspondence between them during the courtship period indicate that Williams harboured anxieties over his sense of class inferiority; he was acutely aware of his lack of higher education in comparison to his future wife.[25] But another, even more problematic reason, underlay his reluctance, as indicated by the most extraordinary letter of all from this period, from E. Prosser Rhys, poet and journalist, to Kate Roberts. On 21 November 1928, a month before the wedding, Rhys wrote:

Nid wyf yn gobeithio y byddwch fyw'n hapus; ni all artist fyw bywyd hapus, yn ystyr gyffredin y gair, beth bynnag. Ond hyderaf y cewch fywyd dwfn, llawn. Peidiwch â disgwyl gormod oddiwrth y bywyd priodasol. Gellwch ddisgwyl llawer o ddiddanwch cnawd ac ysbryd, llawer iawn. Ond na ddisgwyliwch ormod.

(I don't wish you a happy life; an artist cannot live a happy life, in the usual sense of the word, anyway. But I trust you will have a deep, full life. Don't expect too much from married life. You can expect a great deal of physical and spiritual pleasure, a great deal. But don't expect too much).[26]

The subtext of this letter is the source of what must have been a very painful realization for the newly married Kate Roberts. Prosser Rhys had a particular reason for advising her not to 'expect too much' from her marriage, since he himself had been involved in a passionate homosexual relationship with her husband, Morris T. Williams, for a number of years. It is difficult to imagine that Roberts would not have been aware of this but she perhaps felt that her husband's evident feeling for her (in a telling photograph of the time, a flapper-like, bespectacled Roberts gazes adoringly at her young husband, and he smiles serenely back at her) would displace all earlier attachments and even a different sexual orientation. She would certainly not have been the first woman to have felt so, nor to have taken on the challenge of such a marriage.

It is also noteworthy that Morris T. Williams was younger than his wife by roughly the same number of years as was her beloved, late younger brother, who had died just over a decade before. Notable also is the fact that female characters in Roberts's fiction often feel passionate attachments to men who are considerably younger than themselves, sometimes their own brothers, as does the character Ann Owen in the 1958 autobiographical novel, *Tegwch y Bore*, whose most intense emotion seems to be reserved for her somewhat feckless younger brother, Bobi. It is almost as if, in these relationships, the female character's feeling for the young man is a powerful combination of the maternal and the sexual. Roberts herself was and remained childless, and possibly was unable to have children owing to gynaecological problems (it is known that she underwent a serious operation in 1922 and that she was acquainted with a Liverpool consultant who specialised in 'women's problems').[27] And yet her stories show that children were not only very important to her but that she had a rare insight into their consciousness and points of view. It is not beyond the bounds of possibility that Roberts's attraction to Morris T. Williams was connected to an unacknowledged longing to mother, to nurture and to protect, as she had hoped to do – but failed – for her youngest brother and for her own children. Indeed, it is possible that her husband's sexual ambivalence was part of his attraction for her, echoing as it did the inchoate sexuality of adolescence. Moreover, Roberts's fiction also offers accounts of intense, even erotic relationships between women, as commentators such as Francesca Rhydderch have observed, so that the homoerotic nature of Morris T. Williams's relationship with Prosser Rhys would certainly have been understandable to Kate Roberts the writer, if not forgivable to Kate Williams, the wife.

Marriage at the age of thirty-seven had immediate professional consequences for Kate Roberts. Owing to the legal bar against the employment of married women as teachers in place at the time, she had to relinquish her post as a teacher in Aberdare and the newly married couple moved to Rhiwbina in Cardiff in January 1929. Photographs from the period showing Roberts, Morris T. Williams, Caradog and Mattie Pritchard in the garden of 8 Lon Isaf, Rhiwbina suggest that there was at least a honeymoon period of intense happiness for the couple. However, the extant correspondence shows that Morris T. Williams continued to communicate with his former lover, Prosser Rhys, in passionate terms, and there is an unposted letter (dated 24 August 1927) from him to Rhys suggesting the suicidal despair of a gay young man forced to conceal and deny his sexual orientation.[28]

Nevertheless, the relationship between Kate Roberts and her husband was something considerably more than a sexual or a romantic one. They were dedicated political campaigners, united in their work for Plaid Genedlaethol Cymru, as well as sharing literary interests and ambitions. From 1929 until 1931 they lived in the new 'garden village' of Rhiwbina, which Roberts described in very positive terms, though it did not have the traditional community activities to which she was accustomed. Instead, the newly married couple entertained a troupe of literary visitors, including the novelist Caradog Pritchard and his wife, Mattie, W. J. Gruffydd, R. T. Jenkins and Iorwerth Peate. They also joined a society of 'exiles' from north Wales in Cardiff, calling themselves 'Y Gwyneddigion' (The People from Gwynedd) who enjoyed social activities in the Kardomah cafe in the city. The account Roberts gives of their lives at this time is a joyful one but she also emphasizes that it wasn't all socializing: 'trwy ddarllen llawer fe'm paratoais fy hun ar gyfer ysgrifennu storïau ac yn ystod y cyfnod yma yr ysgrifennais *Laura Jones*' (through reading a great deal I prepared myself for writing stories and it was during this period that I wrote *Laura Jones*).[29] Anyone who has made a living as a teacher will also hear the sense of release in Roberts's remark: although she lost her independent income by having to relinquish her teaching post, she also regained the possibility of reading widely, and not just re-reading those texts that she had to teach from day to day, along with the copious essays and exam scripts of her pupils.

3
Finding a voice: 1928–1946

Before the publication of *Laura Jones* in 1930, though, there appeared a second volume of short stories, entitled *Rhigolau Bywyd* (The Ruts of Life; 1929). This volume includes eight short stories and is dedicated to her husband. At the time of its publication in December 1929, Roberts had been married to Morris T. Williams for just a year. It is intriguing, therefore, to find that marriage is at the heart of this collection, just as the parent-child bond was central to Roberts's first volume, dedicated to her parents. Marriage is by no means seen in a positive light here, though; on the contrary, many of the stories concern the loss of romance after marriage. Indeed, in story after story there is a focus on disillusionment and disappointment, tracing particularly the deterioration of intense passion into stolid routine. The title story, for example, explores the way in which work has taken over the lives of Dafydd and Beti Gruffydd: on the day of Dafydd's seventieth birthday, on which he goes to work in the quarry as usual and later works trashing brambles in the fields, Beti has an unwonted epiphany in which she perceives the narrowness and futility of their joyless lives of labour. The story is bleak and foreshadows Dafydd's death, expressed in a vivid snatch of figurative language: 'Sbonciai'r brigau drain fel *Jac-yn-y-bocs*, a disgynnent â'u breichiau ar led i farw yn y ffos' (The brambles jumped up like a jack-in-the-box and then fell down with their arms spread wide to die in the ditch).[1] Such a sentence speaks volumes of the succinctness and symbolic power of Roberts's early writing: the image of the jack-in-the-box suggests the manic yet monotonous movement of the elderly couple's working lives, the mechanical jerkiness and the alienation of labour, while the thorns of the brambles and the outspread arms connote a bitter martyrdom.

Another story in the volume, 'Y Golled' (The Loss), appears to be closer to the experience of Roberts herself, since it concerns a younger couple, married for just eighteen months. Again, the central consciousness of the story is the wife, Annie, who is bitter and sad at the loss of her lover, Ted, who has turned into 'Mr Williams', the phlegmatic husband. The consonance of surnames between the character and Kate Roberts's spouse can hardly be accidental. In the story, Annie manages to persuade the stolid Ted to take a bus trip into the mountains on a Sunday, in hope of rekindling some of the romance of their days of courtship. The beautiful landscape fulfills her expectations but, sadly, Ted does not, for when they return from their idyllic trip, on hearing that some petty excitement had occurred in the Sunday school, Ted wishes he had been there, instead of out in the mountains with Annie. We are left at the end of the story with the discomfiting spectacle of Annie laughing hysterically while Ted looks on, bewildered.[2] The husband and wife live together, yet they inhabit different worlds; he espouses a small-town, small-minded Nonconformist Wales, while she longs, unrealistically and in vain, for a more socially unrestricted, wilder, more romantic place.

The next story again switches from youth to age. 'Rhwng Dau Damaid o Gyfleth' (Between Two Pieces of Toffee) focuses on an old man watching his daughter and granddaughter making toffee, remembering a scene of sixty years before when he had watched his first love, Geini, a servant girl, making toffee with her mistress in exactly the same way. Dafydd remembers in intense and sensuous detail his love affair with Geini, which fails eventually because of her refusal to submit to marriage. She escapes because she realizes that marriage will spell the end of their joy: 'unwaith y priodwn ni, mi awn yr un fath â phawb arall' (once we marry we'll become the same as everyone else).[3] Geini and Annie can be seen as two versions of possible futures that Roberts herself might have chosen: for so long independent (like Annie, who had professional status as a Post Office clerk) she is now married and, one might suppose, finding it difficult to adjust to the new status of being 'Mrs Williams', rather than Miss Roberts the rather formidable, independent schoolteacher, one of 'the three BAs'.

The story entitled 'Nadolig' (Christmas) in the volume also turns on marriage: Olwen is about to accept her lover, Gwilym's, proposal and is happy but also afflicted by guilt because she feels that she is betraying her friendship with an older woman, Miss Davies, with whom she has become intimate. Again, amidst the trappings of Christmas in the town, Olwen has a moment of epiphany when she realizes the nature of Miss Davies's regard for her and her joy is spoilt by the thought of the older woman, bereft, reading her letter explaining her decision to marry. This is by no means the only story where Kate Roberts touches on the intensity of female relationships – her later novella, *Tywyll Heno* (Dark Tonight), also features such a bond – and, given the reticence of her treatment of sex generally, this aspect of Roberts's work can be regarded as fairly daring in the Welsh context. Olwen sympathizes with the older woman intensely, realizing that 'felly y byddai hithau ryw ddiwrnod efallai' (she would herself be like her one day, perhaps).[4] The two women have shared the dubious joys of schoolteaching together, the 'free hour' in the middle of the school day memorably described as 'awr o arllwys inc coch fel gwaed llofruddiaethau hyd gopïau plant' (an hour of pouring red ink like murderous blood all over children's copybooks).[5] By the end of the story, all the accoutrements of Christmas in the street have turned into a great slaughterhouse of dead animals for Olwen, oppressed by her betrayal and figurative 'murder' of her female friend.

A different female relationship is at the heart of another story, 'Chwiorydd' (Sisters). Again, this is a story that paints a bleak picture of marriage since, when Meri Ifans has several strokes and becomes unable to look after herself, her husband John neglects her shamefully, as does her daughter, but her sister, Sara, sees to her needs and keeps her clean. True to Roberts's habitual represen-tation of housework as something that often gives meaning and purpose to women's narrow lives, this is a story of sisterly love which is manifested in the triumph of keeping a narrow circle clean amid a filthy and neglected household.

'Meddyliau Siopwr' (A Shopkeeper's Thoughts) is something of a departure for Kate Roberts stylistically, since it takes the form of an interior monologue in the first-person voice of a shop-keeper who appears to be suffering a nervous breakdown. The protagonist is angry and obsessive, his voice increasingly hysterical; the story indicates Roberts's abiding interest in mental illness, one which will receive fuller and more successful treatment in the later novella, *Tywyll Heno*. This collection also includes another more experimental, impressionistic story, entitled 'Y Gwynt' (The Wind), which Francesca Rhydderch suggests may be seen as Roberts's emulation of Virginia Woolf's Modernist style. Certainly, Roberts admired Woolf's work and even suggested in a later radio interview that 'mae un awdur Saesneg y byddaf yn gweld y gellid efelychu ei dull yn y Gymraeg, sef Miss Virginia Woolf' (there is one English writer I see that it would be possible to emulate her style in Welsh, namely Miss Virginia Woolf).[6] But, as Rhydderch notes, Welsh critics were less than enthusiastic in their reception of this particular story, with even the normally enthusiastic Derec Llwyd Morgan deeming it to be 'a bit fanci-ful'.[7] 'Y Gwynt' is also a first-person narrative, in which the un-named male narrator comes to stay in a hotel in Caersaint on a windy night. The story is then taken over by the sound of the wind, which mutates into the voice of a long-dead woman who tells her sad story of blighted love and suicide. There is a rare self-consciousness about this story which certainly does indicate that Roberts was experimenting with a style far removed from her usual realism: at the end of the story, for instance, the spectral voice asks 'Ydych chi wedi blino ar fy stori?'; the narrator answers 'Ydwyf' (Are you tired of my story/ Yes I am), and the story, as if responding to a readerly verdict, comes to an end.[8]

D. J. Williams, a fellow writer whose opinion she valued, wrote to Roberts to express his admiration of *Rhigolau Bywyd*, suggest-ing that it was better than *O Gors y Bryniau*, more mature and more succinct. He singles out 'Between Two Pieces of Toffee' as the best story,[9] as does Margaret Price, her former collaborator on the dramatic pieces of the early twenties, who also admires 'The Loss'. It is interesting here to reflect that Roberts might have developed in a different direction stylistically had the reception in Wales of her more experimental, Modernist works been more positive. In the event, she dedicated herself to a realist mode for the rest of her writing career, a mode which Francesca Rhydderch has called 'a politically rigorous anti-modernis[m] rather than a provincially unfashionable realis[m]'.[10] Roberts did experiment with versions of Modernism, as we have seen, but she shared with Raymond Williams a wariness of the potential solipsism of Modernist subjectivity. Yet, we also know that she admired the work of prominent Modernists, notably Mansfield, Woolf and Joyce, as well as the proto-Modernist Chekhov. She is reticent with regard to sexual relationships and acts in her fiction, which she herself acknowledged in interviews, putting it down to the kind of upbringing she experienced. In the 1920s, this reticence perhaps made her seem old-fashioned in comparison with the frankness of contemporaries such as D. H. Lawrence, Joyce and Anaïs Nin but, on the other hand, fellow writers such as Woolf and Mansfield were equally coy when it came to sexual explicitness. Indeed, Roberts's reticence could be regarded as being as much an aspect of the indirection and subtlety of her style as it is a defect of her repressive chapel education. Whatever reasons a critic may adduce for her ultimate rejection of Modernism, one thing can be asserted with certainty: it was not because she was ignorant of the Modernist innovations that were happening in world literature that she failed to espouse them. On the contrary, she was very well aware of contemporary developments in literature and kept a sharp and invariably judgmental eye on the work of her peers in the late 1920s and 1930s.

But there was some unfinished business to be published, in the form of *Laura Jones*, which looked back inevitably towards the earlier *Deian a Loli*, rather than looking forwards with a more distinctive aesthetic as the stories of *Rhigolau Bywyd* do. Despite Iorwerth C. Peate's negative reception of *Laura Jones* in his review which was, according to Roberts herself, enough to make a cat laugh, other critics and readers were more favourably inclined. D. J. Williams, for example, wrote to Roberts in January 1931 expressing his appreciation of the work, which he praised as being as beautiful as a poem. He had read Saunders Lewis's shocking novel, *Monica*, at about the same time, he confesses, but was glad that he read *Laura Jones* after *Monica*, since it 'took some of the smell of cat piss away'.[11] However, despite Williams's praise, *Laura Jones* is an uneven and unstable text generically. It is a sequel to *Deian and Loli*, recounting Loli's experiences after she leaves home and goes into service. Similar material is covered much more ambitiously in Roberts's later stories about the character Winni Ffinni Hadog. The hand of the schoolmistress lies rather too heavily upon *Laura Jones* at times: it includes a glossary and an unnecessary justification of non-grammatical usage in the characters' speech, for instance. The reader is left wondering why other characters are so entranced by Loli and why she is seen as being so unusual. Nevertheless, there are interesting aspects to this novel, which hovers between being addressed to adults and children. The representation of Nain, an old lady who is clearly suffering from dementia, is poignant and unsentimental. She and Loli strike up an unexpected rapport; the old woman empathizes with Loli in all the hard physical labour she is forced to do. It suddenly reminds her of her own youth in service, when she had to get up at four in the morning on washing day. She pointedly remarks that Wil, the boy servant who worked with her, always thanked God that he hadn't been born a girl. But Loli is the central focus; she is a Robertsian alter ego – what the author might have been if she had not received an education (which, in the text, is bestowed upon her twin brother, Deian). Loli grows into her official name, Laura Jones, and is aware of the shift in her identity, from childhood to adulthood, from dependent daughter to independent worker. At the end of the novella, Laura Jones is poised to reinvent herself as a writer or newspaper journalist, an ambition which interestingly foreshadows Kate Roberts's own trajectory towards running a publishing house.

Indeed, it is in this period of the early 1930s that political journalism and activism begin to play an increasingly significant role in Roberts's life. However disillusioned she may have felt with the institution of marriage, she was and remained unswervingly committed to it, and that commitment became at this time intertwined with her commitment to the Welsh language and nationalist politics. For some years after her marriage, politics threatened to take centre stage in her life. From Rhiwbina, Roberts and her husband moved to Tonypandy in the Rhondda valley in the summer of 1931 and the next four years became a period of intense campaigning on behalf of the Plaid Genedlaethol for the couple, as they gradually gathered around them a small group of similarly engaged nationalist activists. Monthly visits to Cardiff widened their circle of friends and acquaintances. Morris T. Williams stood as a Plaid candidate in local elections and Kate Roberts threw herself with characteristic vigour into canvassing and campaigning on his behalf. Williams stood unsuccessfully three times in a row, a dispiriting experience for both; Roberts was particularly disillusioned by the smug and dismissive attitudes of the Labour Party activists and candidates whom she met on the campaign trail. (One wonders what she would have made of the current situation in the Welsh Assembly government, which is a coalition between Labour and Plaid Cymru.) In pounding the streets on behalf of the party, Roberts gained a first-hand view of the poverty of the Rhondda at the time: the many families living in a single house, the lack of food and clothing and, an important point for Roberts, the people's lack of the Welsh language and their ignorance of its culture. Roberts did try to do something to help. She distributed children's clothing to needy families, for example, clothes that had been knitted and sent to her by students at Aberystwyth.[12]

In 1931, Roberts again tried her hand at drama, this time without the two female collaborators with whom she had written the comedies of the early 1920s. She wrote a play entitled *Ffarwel i Addysg* (Farewell to Education), which she submitted unsuccessfully to the drama competition in the 1931 National Eisteddfod at

Bangor. Despite not winning the competition, the play was performed, having its debut in the Canon Lewis Memorial Hall in Pentre in the Rhondda in December 1932. One can see why it did not win the competition. The dialogue is stilted and rather too literary, while the characters themselves are surprisingly un-engaging. Nevertheless, from a feminist point of view, it is a fascinating text, a kind of Cymric *Doll's House*, in which the main protagonist, Gwen, risks all and loses for the sake of her love for Dafydd, yet when she is expelled from her college and Dafydd is eager to 'do the decent thing' and marry her, she refuses. It is a strange play for a newly married woman to write, perhaps. It is almost as if Roberts is revisiting her own youth and exploring alternative paths in life.

It was while Kate Roberts and her husband were still living at 7 Kenry Street in Tonypandy that Roberts wrote, in late 1933, a fan letter to Vera Brittain, whose autobiographical work, *Testament of Youth*, about her experiences during the First World War, had moved her deeply. Brittain wrote warmly in return, mentioning that she must have worked as a nurse in Malta at the same time that Roberts's brother was in hospital there. Brittain thoughtfully mentions the loveliness of the Pietà cemetery in Malta, where Dei Roberts was buried: 'you could not wish for him to be buried in any more beautiful place'.[13] Both women writers seem united in their determination to prevent their countries from, as Brittain puts it, 'being dragged into another imperialist war'. Even more interestingly, Brittain's letter reveals that Roberts is working on 'a long novel', which we can only surmise must be *Traed mewn Cyffion* (Feet in Chains), a work that, to an extent, can be regarded as Kate Roberts's *Testament of Youth*.

Although writing *Traed mewn Cyffion* was taking her back in her memory and imagination to the Caernarfonshire of her youth, it is clear that Roberts was very much concerned by the hardship of the people of the Rhondda in the midst of the Depression. One indication of this is the essay she published in *Y Traethodydd* (The Essayist) in April 1935. Entitled 'Dianc' (Escape), the essay focuses on the lack of engagement of contemporary Welsh literature with the reality of life in the Rhondda at the time. Roberts speaks urgently in the first person, bearing witness to the extreme poverty in the streets where she herself lives. She contrasts the present with the years of the First World War, which did produce a literary response in Welsh, a literature, she says, to 'warm the blood'. But the suffering of that time was public, visible, common to all classes, unlike the miserable, hidden suffering of contemporary poverty. She concludes, sadly 'Peth diramant yw tlodi' (Poverty is an un-romantic thing). She accuses contemporary writers in Welsh of escaping into the past and of belonging to a new middle class with little direct experience of the effects of the Depression, while the sufferers themselves have lost their Welsh and its culture, and so are unable to tell their own stories. No solution to the problem is offered and, tellingly, Roberts includes herself in the condemnation of escapist authors.[14]

While Kate Roberts came from a poor background and, later in life, in the post-Second World War period suffered from severe money shortages, in the early 1930s, she and her husband must have counted themselves relatively well off, particularly in com-parison with their neighbours in Tonypandy. In 1935, though, they decided to move back to north Wales and to take on a new venture. Williams was a master printer by trade, so it made sense for them to become partners in this major project: the buying and running of Gwasg Gee, a well-known publishing house, in Denbigh. This meant a move back to their native north Wales for both. They had the money to buy the press and, as Nia Williams notes, their new home, Y Cilgwyn, where Roberts would live for the rest of her life, was designed and built to Roberts's own specifi-cations based on an 'Ideal Home' design.[15] Their furniture was of Welsh oak, made by Morris T. Williams's carpenter brother, while even the bathroom taps 'spoke' Welsh, offering 'poeth' and 'oer' water, rather than 'hot' and 'cold.' For Kate Roberts the creative writer, though, this move was the beginning of a period of silence, as she dedicated her formidable energies firstly to making the press a successful business and, secondly, to writing for *Baner ac Amserau Cymru* (The Banner and Times of Wales), the newspaper that they took over at Gwasg Gee in the late 1930s. For a while, Kate Roberts the short story writer, novelist and playwright would be transformed into Kate Roberts the businesswoman and journalist.

But just before that shift in her work and world came a final flourish of creative fiction from the first period of her writing life. In 1936, the novel for which she is still best known was published, *Traed mewn Cyffion*, though it was submitted to the 1934 National Eisteddfod and must therefore have been written in 1932–3, well before the move back to north Wales. After several failures in Eisteddfod competitions in the past, Roberts must have been glad to win the Prose Medal at the National Eisteddfod for this novel, though she had to share the prize with another female novelist, Grace Wynne Griffith. Gerwyn Wiliams makes an interesting comparison between *Traed mewn Cyffion* and *Creigiau Milgwyn* (The Rocks of Milgwyn), the novel by Grace Wynne Griffith with which it shared the Prose Medal, concluding that the latter is a 'feminine' novel, while Kate Roberts's is a 'masculine' novel.[16] This observation begs a number of questions. It is unlikely that a critic of Wiliams's calibre is simply making a misogynist generalization; that is, because Roberts's novel is obviously superior in literary terms, it must therefore be deemed 'masculine'. I believe Wiliams is making a point about genre: *Traed mewn Cyffion* does not take the form of a romance, which is still regarded as a predominantly 'feminine' form, whereas Griffith's novel does. That Roberts was capable of resorting to a version of romance is evidenced by her later novel, *Tegwch y Bore*,[17] but it is true that on the whole she either avoids or subverts the conventional romance genre which was more or less prescribed for Welsh female writers of her generation, perhaps partly as a consequence of the immense popular success of the romance fiction of the Anglo-Welsh novelist, Allen Raine.[18]

The set task for the competition in the 1934 National Eisteddfod was a novel about three generations; both Roberts and Grace Griffith responded by writing a family saga. *Creigiau Milgwyn* is about three times as long as *Traed mewn Cyffion* and is the author's first and – as far as I have been able to determine – only novel. The author's inexperience shows in the clunky and over-detailed exposition, while her language, though perfectly serviceable, lacks the brilliant succinctness and command of idiom which characterizes Roberts's work. It is also excessively Anglicized at times, for example, in a phrase such as 'gwelsant y ferch gyntaf yn yr ardal yn mentro "ridicule" trwy reidio beic' (they saw the first girl in the neighbourhood risking 'ridicule' by riding a bike).[19] Griffith's novel bristles with the clichés of romance and frequently lapses into sentiment; on the other hand, she dares to treat some topics on which Roberts is silent, for example a long and painful labour endured by one of the characters, Ann, in giving birth to a baby daughter. Nevertheless, it is difficult to understand how the Eisteddfod judge, Tom Richards, could have considered Griffith's novel equal to Roberts's; presumably, he wished to reward and encourage the apprentice writer's ambition.

Traed mewn Cyffion was first published by Gwasg Aberystwyth in 1936. This press was established and run by E. Prosser Rhys, and Roberts dedicates the novel to him. This indicates that the passionate friendship that he and Morris T. Williams shared was not a barrier to Kate Roberts's also regarding him as a friend, one close enough to merit a dedication in perhaps her most significant work. The close connection of the three was intensified by their increasing business and professional links, with Rhys being editor of *Baner ac Amserau Cymru* which Gwasg Gee published. Roberts and Williams supported their friend's own publishing venture, Gwasg Aberystwyth; all three were dedicated to widening the scope of Welsh-language publishing and championing the reading and circulation of Welsh books. Rhys must have been delighted to be publishing a novel which he, as an astute critic and journalist as well as a gifted poet, must have recognized as a classic.

Traed mewn Cyffion is set in the slate quarrying/smallholding community of Caernarfonshire between the 1880s and the end of the First World War. It focuses on the people of Moel Arian, who live a life of austerity, incessant labour and rigid self-discipline. The novel draws attention to their stoicism but at the same time shows how enchained they are both by their sense of duty and by their political naivety. It is a novel that combines an intimate picture of a single family with a panoramic and synoptic view of a Wales undergoing the changes that would bring it into the modern world. The central figure in the novel is Jane Gruffydd who, at the beginning of the narrative, is a newly married young woman who has recently moved to the slate-quarrying region of Moel Arian from her remote home on the Llŷn Peninsula. The atmospheric opening passage of the novel is among the best known of twentieth-century texts to readers of the Welsh language:

Sŵn pryfed, sŵn eithin yn clecian, sŵn gwres, a llais y pregethwr yn sïo ymlaen yn felfedaidd. Oni bai ei fod allan yn yr awyr agored buasai'n drymllyd, a buasai mwy na hanner y gynulleidfa'n cysgu. Dyma'r Sul ym Mehefin pan gynhaliai Methodistiaid Moel Arian eu cyfarfod pregethu. Gan fod y capel yn fychan a'r dynfa i gyfarfodydd pregethu yn 1880 yn un gref, cynhelid ef ar gae. Cludid y pregethwr ymlaen ar lanw ei huodledd ei hun. Yr oedd popeth yn fanteisiol iddo; tyrfa fawr o'i flaen; tywydd tawel, poeth; cantel yr awyr yn las ac yn bell; y môr yntau'n las ar y gorwel; a chylch o fynyddoedd y tu cefn iddo . . . yr oedd llygaid llawer arno, y rhai oedd ar flaen y dyrfa; ond yr oedd anniddigrwydd ar y cyrion, ymhlith y merched gan mwyaf, eu hesgidiau newydd yn eu gwasgu, eu staesiau newydd yn rhy dynn, a choleri uchel ei ffrogiau newydd yn eu mygu . . . Un o'r rhai hyn oedd Jane Gruffydd, oedd newydd briodi ag Ifan, mab y Fawnog. Yr oedd hi ers meityn bron â griddfan o eisiau mynd adref. Yr oedd ei gwasg gyda'r meinaf o ferched y gynulleidfa, ar draul tynnu mawr ar garrai ei staes cyn cychwyn i'r oedfa. Ei thimpan hi oedd y fwyaf ar y cae, sidan ei ffrog hi oedd y trymaf a'r sythaf yno, ganddi hi yr oedd mwyaf o ffrils ar ei ffrog a'r bluen drymaf ar ei het. Yr oedd llygaid llawer o'r merched arni hi, oblegid gan ychydig iawn ohonynt yr oedd ffrog sidan a safai ar ei phen.[20]

(The sound of insects humming, the sound of the gorse cracking, the sound of heat rising, and the velvety voice of the preacher murmuring on and on. If it hadn't been out in the open air it would have felt close, and more than half the congregation would have fallen asleep. This was the Sunday in June when the Methodists of Moel Arian held their prayer meeting. Since the chapel was small and the attraction of prayer meetings in 1880 a powerful one, it was held out in a field. The preacher was borne onward by the tide of his own eloquence. Every-thing was in his favour: a large crowd before him; warm, calm weather; the rim of the sky far off and blue; the sea itself blue all the way to the horizon; and a circle of mountains as a backdrop behind him . . . many eyes were upon him, the eyes of those at the front of the crowd; but there was discontent at the edges, especially among the women, whose new shoes were pinching, their new stays too tight, and the high collars of their new frocks stifling . . . One of the latter was Jane Gruffydd, who had recently married Ifan, the son of Y Fawnog. For some time now she had been almost whimpering in her longing to go home. Her waist was one of the smallest among the women in the congregation, as a result of much tugging at the cords of her stays before she started her way to the service. Her bustle was the largest in the field, the satin of her dress was the heaviest and stiffest there, it was she who had the most frills on her frock and the heaviest feather on her hat. Many of the women's eyes were upon her, since very few of them owned a satin dress which could stand up on its own.)

This opening, with its rhythmical, poetic phrasing, strikes a different stylistic note from that heard in Roberts's previous work as a short story writer. It is clear that she is aware of the larger scale of this work, and she starts as she means to go on, with a description which confidently takes in the whole extensive scene: preacher, congregation, mountain, sea, horizon. But what is more impressive still is the way in which this first-time novelist confidently shifts the centre of interest from the preacher, who is gently mocked for his self-importance, to the women chafing at the edges of the crowd, bored by the clergyman's self-indulgent eloquence and tortured by their elaborately constrictive, late Victorian garments. Jane Gruffydd is positioned as a female counterpart to the pontifi-cating minister balanced on the cart which is his makeshift pulpit; she is the object of the collective female gaze, her finery much more eye-catching and fascinating than any rhetorical flights of fancy in the preacher's interminable sermon.

The setting of the novel soon shifts to the domestic sphere where Jane is, again, at the centre. We witness her getting to grips with hand-washing her quarryman husband's work clothes while also coping with the criticism of her mother-in-law. As the years pass,

Jane gives birth to six children and we see her transform from the proud young fashion-plate of the opening to what Francesca Rhydderch has resonantly called an 'Everymam'.[21] Roberts uses this one family as a microcosm of Wales, revealing its increasing Anglicization, secularization and migration through different members of the Gruffydd family. The 'chains' of the title are seen fettering the characters in different ways: the strongest fetters are the economic ones – poverty and vulnerability to the whims of capital. Wiliam, the politically engaged son, leaves home to join the unionized labour of the south Wales coal mines because he is disillusioned with his fellow quarrymen, whom he sees as being content to 'caress the chains of their enslavement' ('roedd yn well ganddynt lyfu cadwynau eu caethiwed').[22]

Gradually, the centre of consciousness in the novel shifts from Jane to her son, Owen, a scholarship boy of the same generation as the author herself. Owen reflects on the chains of the family itself, its constant demand for loyalty, its pressure on the individual to do his duty, to persevere, to perpetuate the line of stoical sufferers: 'peth mor rhyfedd oedd teulu. Edrychai darluniau rhai ohonynt arno yn awr oddi ar y parwydydd. Byddai arno awydd i'w malu weithiau er mwyn anghofio ei dras. Ac eto, yr oedd yn amhosibl ymddihatru oddi wrthynt' (family was such a strange thing. Portraits of some of them hanging on the walls looked down on him now. Sometimes he felt a strong urge to smash them up in order to be able to forget his lineage. And yet, it was impossible to disentangle himself from them).[23] Clearly, Roberts is using the Gruffydd family here partly as an allegory of Welshness, and the burden that places on the individual, a burden which, despite her strong ideological commitment, she herself often felt. As she once complained, only slightly tongue-in-cheek: 'Mae hi'n drist meddwl mai'r rhai a fedrai ddarparu llenyddiaeth i Gymru sy'n gorfod ceisio achub ei henaid' (It's sad to think that it's those who could provide Wales with literature who have to try to save her soul).[24]

By the last five chapters in the novel, the First World War has thrown its shadow over the community of Moel Arian. As I have argued elsewhere, the war is used to indicate a decisive shift in the history of this society and, ironically enough, suggests the possibility of escape from the multiple chains that bind them. The novel demonstrates how an awareness of subjection begins to grow in the general consciousness and it is the war which, unexpectedly, effects this political awakening. When Twm, one of the sons of Ffridd Felen joins up, his family is at first shocked by his betrayal of family duty: 'A dyma Twm yn gwneud tro mor wael! Pan allasai anfon ychydig arian adref, yn mynd at y soldiwrs' (here was Twm playing such a shabby trick! When he could be sending a little money home each month, he had gone and joined the army).[25] Soon, though, the shocking news comes that Twm is to be sent to France. Gradually, the people of Moel Arian begin to awake from their stoical quietism:

A dechreuodd y bobl oedd gartref eu holi eu hunain a holi ei gilydd beth oedd ystyr peth fel hyn . . . Ni chredent o gwbl erbyn hyn mai achub cam gwledydd bychain oedd amcan y Rhyfel, ac mai rhyfel i orffen rhyfel ydoedd . . . daethant i gredu bod pobl ym mhob gwlad oedd yn dda ganddynt ryfel, a'u bod yn defnyddio eu bechgyn hwy i'w mantais eu hunain. 'Y bobol fawr' yna oedd y rhai hynny, yr un bobl a wasgai arnynt yn y chwarel, ac a sugnai eu gwaed a'i droi'n aur iddynt hwy eu hunain . . . Siglai eu ffydd mewn pregethwyr a gwladweinwyr . . . Ond âi'r Rhyfel ymlaen.[26]

(They began to ask what was the meaning of it all . . . They did not believe at all now that the war was being fought to save the smaller nations, or that it was a war to end all wars . . .They came to realize that, in every country, there were people who regarded war as a good thing, and were taking advantage of their sons to promote their own interests. These were 'The Ruling Class', the same people who oppressed them in the quarry, who sucked their blood and turned it into gold for themselves . . . their views began to change. Their faith in preachers and politicians was shaken . . . But the war continued).

Jane Gruffydd, the Everymam, also awakes from her stoical torpor by the end of the novel. Having been informed of her son Twm's death in an official letter written in a language, English, which she is unable to read, she begins to feel a growing anger and resentment against the state which has senselessly robbed her of a son. She physically attacks the smug military pensions officer who intrudes into her domestic space:

> Y munud hwnnw daeth rhyw deimlad rhyfedd dros Jane Gruffydd. Ers pymtheg mis o amser, bu rhyw deimladau yn crynhoi yn ei henaid yn erbyn pob dim oedd yn gyfrifol am y Rhyfel, yn erbyn dynion ac yn erbyn Duw; a phan welodd y dyn blonegog yma yn ei ddillad graenus yn gorfoleddu am dynnu pensiwn gwraig weddw dlawd i lawr, methodd ganddi ddal. Yr oedd fel casgliad yn torri, y dyn yma a gynrychiolai bob dim oedd y tu ôl i'r Rhyfel ar y munud hwnnw, a dyma hi'n cipio'r peth nesaf i law – brws dillad oedd hwnnw – a tharo'r swyddog yn ei ben.
> 'Cerwch allan o'r tŷ yma, mewn munud,' meddai.[27]

> (At that moment a strange feeling came over Jane Gruffydd. For fifteen long months, a deep resentment had been gathering in her very soul against everything that was responsible for the war, against man and against God. And when she saw this plump man in his immaculate clothes preening himself on the fact that he had reduced a widow's pension, she lost control of herself. It was like a dam bursting. At that moment, the man standing before her represented all that was behind the War. She grabbed the nearest thing to hand – a clothes-brush – and struck him on the head with it. 'Get out of this house at once,' she shouted.)

It is Owen, who belongs to Roberts's own generation, who has the final vision: 'ac fe agorwyd ei lygaid i bosibilrwydd gwneud rhywbeth, yn lle dioddef fel mudion' (his eyes were opened to the possibility of doing something instead of simply enduring like a dumb animal).[28] The novel shows a nationalist and a socialist consciousness being born in the people of one corner of Wales as a direct result of their bitter experience of war. Historians of Plaid Cymru, founded, as we have seen, in the mid-1920s, concur that war experiences greatly influenced the nationalist feeling which gave rise to the party. Particularly galling for many was the idea that the war was allegedly fought, as the novel puts it, to 'help the small nations', a slogan which naturally encouraged many young Welsh people to join up. Emblematically, near the end of the novel, the archetypal Everymam takes up her brush not to scrub and scour but to attack the representative of the oppressive British state, which extends its tentacles even as far as her own domestic hearth. It is also emblematic that the novel begins with a scene of community: hundreds of people joined together in the open air prayer meeting, whereas it ends with a solitary young man, questioning and wondering what the future might hold for himself and his people.

In a letter of 6 May 1936, Saunders Lewis writes to thank Roberts for *Traed mewn Cyffion*, which he has enjoyed reading much more the second time around. He commends the excellent Welsh which reminds him, he says, of some very special local wine in France, a wine which you have to go to the place where they grow the vines in order to appreciate its worth – Jurançon 1924, for example – with the taste of the Pyrenees in every drop. He concludes by saying that writing of that order is an act of 'am-ddiffyniad i'r genedl' (defence of the nation).[29] *Traed mewn Cyffion* is available in an English translation, which first appeared in the late 1970s but, it has to be admitted, that the taste of that fine Jurançon 1924 becomes slightly vinegary in English translation. As the novelist Emyr Humphreys comments, despite the best efforts of translators, sometimes the expected miracle just does not happen.[30] Roberts is difficult to translate: her succinct, laconic and often dialectal language can come across as flat in an over-literal English. Fortunately, though, in recent years, many more of Roberts's works have appeared in English translation, often in versions by authors who are creative writers themselves, such as the current national poet of Wales, Gillian Clarke, and the distinguished novelist, Siân James.

Ffair Gaeaf a Storïau Eraill (1937) was published by Gwasg Gee in Denbigh and dedicated to Saunders Lewis, for 'his greatness as a man and a writer' ('i'w fawredd fel dyn a llenor'). This was the first volume of Roberts's own creative work to be published by the press she and her husband had newly acquired, and in fact it would be the last for another dozen years. The volume also speaks of its time in its dedication to Saunders Lewis, who had, in the previous year, along with Roberts's other close friends, D. J. Williams and Lewis Valentine, performed the act of civil disobedience that has come to be known as 'the burning of the bombing school'. The three nationalists were put on trial for their attempt to sabotage the military defence establishment that was being built on the Llŷn Peninsula at Penyberth and, to cut a lengthy and dramatic saga short, were eventually imprisoned in Wormwood Scrubs. Thus, Roberts's dedication to Saunders for his 'greatness as a man and as a writer' is a pointed statement of political, personal and literary solidarity.

The collection consists of nine short stories, several of them among Roberts's best-known works and one, 'Y Condemniedig', (The Condemned) considered by many, including the author herself, as her masterpiece. Three of the stories are set in the south Wales mining valleys during the Depression of the 1930s, the others in Roberts's native north-west Wales, two of them in the nineteenth century.

Roberts is clearly drawing on her own recent personal experience of witnessing the poverty and hardship of the south Wales valleys in the 1930s in these stories. Although there is considerable evidence that she was less than happy in the south Wales valleys and felt homesick for her native 'square mile' in the north, her fiction of the south certainly reveals her empathy for the people of the area, and her admiration of their strength and endurance. Her rendition of their speech also shows her keen ear for dialectal difference; her Rhondda characters speak with an authentic accent. Roberts's narrative voice does appear more distant in these stories, and yet she is as astute and perceptive as ever in her observation of familial relationships, domestic interiors and the interaction between people and place. Moreover, her mature style by this stage in her career is an instrument of great subtlety and flexibility; she deploys free indirect style to wander from consciousness to consciousness among her characters, offering brilliant, ironic insights into the differing perspectives of husband and wife, father and daughter, mother and son. These stories, with their unflinching examination of economic hardship, poverty and the desperate struggle to survive with dignity can be seen as Roberts's own response to the challenge laid down in her 1935 essay, 'Dianc', in which, as we have seen, she accused Welsh writers of escaping from this distressing contemporary reality.

'Buddugoliaeth Alaw Jim' begins in a quasi-proverbial style, somewhat reminiscent of Caradoc Evans's notorious short story, 'Be This Her Memorial': 'Ni ddigwyddasai'r stori hon oni buasai i'r wraig gael y gair cyntaf ar ei gŵr' (This story would not have happened were it not that the wife got the first word before her husband).[31] The somewhat cryptic opening adage is then explained in the events of the story. The contrast here, as in the next story, 'Y Gorymdaith' (The Protest March), is between the different responses of a husband and wife to the unavoidable fact of their poverty and their desperate need. Morgan places his hope and trust in the prowess of his beloved greyhound, called 'Alaw Jim', who has just unexpectedly won a race and a money prize for his delighted owner. But Ann, married to Morgan, feels contempt for her husband's naivety and what she sees as his fecklessness. She is clearly at the end of her tether. Roberts's technique, moving from one perspective to the other, emphasizes the division between husband and wife and their disparate ways of trying to cope with a dire economic situation. Morgan recalls sadly the days of their courtship in the countryside, when Ann was all to him and he composed poems to her. It is another tale of disappointment, disillusion and loss. But it is also, of course, thanks to Alaw Jim's victory, a story of consolation, of hope, of winning through despite everything. When Morgan decides to return to Ann at the end of the story, he has a small epiphany, a moment of personal triumph when he decides to give her the prize money, despite the way she has rejected and derided him. In many ways, this is an archetypal Kate Roberts story in the fine balance it maintains between hope and despair, and the equally delicate balance between husband and wife.

This story is linked to 'Diwrnod i'r Brenin' (Red-letter Day), another south Welsh story, by the unexpected acquisition of a ten shilling note. Here, Wat Watcyn and his daughter, Rachel Annie,

receive the money from an uncle, allowing both to enjoy an unwonted 'red-letter day' of pleasure in the midst of their hardship
and the monotony of their everyday lives. The centre of consciousness in this story is Rachel Annie and we follow her on her day
trip to Cardiff, enjoying with her the unusual delights of tea in a
cafe, flowers bought in the market and window shopping in the
big city, away from the grinding poverty of the valleys. We see
Rachel emerge from the 'paralysis' of her everyday life, the four
endless years of her father's unemployment. But most poignant
is the deftly sketched portrait of the close bond between father
and daughter: Rachel Annie spends most of her money on a gift to
take back to her father, while he carefully prepares tea for her by
the time she arrives back. This is an atmospheric and haunting
story, again, like 'Buddugoliaeth Alaw Jim', affording a central
character a moment of bittersweet self-knowledge, without providing an unrealistic happy ending.

The final story set in the south is 'Y Gorymdaith', which
manages in the space of just seven pages to suggest the whole
history of the Rhondda valley. Roberts succeeds in sketching for
us an extensive historical hinterland by focusing intensely on
one married couple, Bronwen and Idris. Raymond Williams
suggested in his seminal essay, 'The Welsh industrial novel', that
the working-class Welsh novelists of the 1930s used the family as
a microcosm for the whole of a new society, a new 'structure of
feeling'; Kate Roberts does this in *Traed mewn Cyffion*, Williams
notes, but it is also true of her short stories, where the microcosm is
frequently not even the extended family but simply the husband
and wife.[32] Through one couple, Roberts indicates so much, not
just about gender relations, but about the relationship between
the individual and society, the individual and history, duty and
desire, hope and despair. This is one of Roberts's most political
stories, for Bronwen goes on a protest march against the Means
Test, which has been introduced to exacerbate the misery of the
unemployed even further. Bronwen still believes, albeit vestigially,
that there is a point to political action such as this, whereas her
husband, Idris, has lost hope entirely, literally turning his face to

the wall in despair. But Bronwen's hopes are dashed and she returns home after the march with mixed feelings of guilt, humiliation, regret and sadness, which Roberts brilliantly encapsulates in a simile: 'Aeth i mewn fel ci wedi bod yn lladd defaid' (She went in like a dog who has been killing sheep).[33] And yet, even in this sad story, there is a moment of hope in the end; as so often in Roberts's work, this hope is expressed in a domestic gesture of kindness. Idris makes tea for Bronwen, and this simple act suggesting his continuing love, concern and regard for her, his desire to nourish, sustain and console her, gives Bronwen some hope again at the end of the story, after the dispiriting experience of the march itself.

In these stories, Roberts's characters are often hampered by ignorance: Bronwen, for example, is perplexed by the political orator at the protest march because he refers to the proletariat and she does not know the meaning of the word. These characters are suffering individuals whose pain is the more poignant because they themselves do not understand why they find themselves living in poverty and misery. Like the north Welsh characters of her other works, they are able to survive through their heroic stoicism. But stoicism is not enough. There is always a hint that education, a coming to consciousness, an analysis of their own situation in the world is needed for these people to effect a change in their circumstances. And yet there is no triumphant revolution in the pages of Kate Roberts's fiction.

The other stories in the volume include 'Y Cwilt' (The Quilt), a story which revolves around Ffebi Williams, who is, along with her husband, a failed shopkeeper, driven out of business by the advent of the first supermarkets. Once again, the story focuses on failure and loss, for Ffebi and John Williams are forced to auction off virtually all their possessions. Indeed, the device of the auction is one that recurs in Roberts's writing: it is an apt emblem of the Robertsian world, for at an auction everything is reduced to monetary value and to economic transactions, and yet the objects in the auction are the objects which tell the emotional story of a lifetime, perhaps even several generations. The most intense emotion of this story finds its objective correlative in the image of the hand-stitched quilt of the title, one of Ffebi's possessions which remains with her throughout her life, while everything else seems to slip through her fingers. She literally wraps herself in it while her world crumbles around her – and the young removal man, with un-intentional cruelty, laughs at the old woman peeping out from her quilted nest. Once again, Roberts displays her skill in the manipulation of the short story genre; in tracing the contours of one life, she manages to suggest the trajectory of a whole way of life and culture.

'Ffair Gaeaf' (Winter Fair), the title story of the collection, con-sists of a number of interwoven miniature stories involving characters attending the annual winter fair in a small Welsh town, recognizable as Caernarfon. Roberts adopts a Woolfian technique here of focusing on the diverse inhabitants of a railway carriage en route to town: the characters, old, young, male, female, married or single, pursue their desires and pleasures but are, largely, disappointed. The fair itself is not what it was; it remains as a vestige of a once vibrant, traditional rural life, degenerate and ana-chronistic in the modern age. Instead of the home-made cakes and cheeses and the ballad-singers of old, the characters find themselves bathed in the unromantic glare of the electric street lights, drinking tea from aluminium teapots.

'Dwy Storm' (Two Storms) shares a similar structure to the earlier 'Between Two Pieces of Toffee', since it juxtaposes the 'now' of an old man's life with a point many years before when the course of his life changed decisively. Just as the piece of toffee functioned in the earlier story as a Proustian madeleine, recalling earlier experiences, in this story a storm in nature brings to mind a similar storm many years before, and the human turmoil that went along with it. Eban Llwyd, a retired quarryman, is snow-bound in his remote cottage for twelve days. This enforced isolation makes him remember the loss of his beloved, Aels, who left him for another man thirty-four years before. The lonely and embittered Eban, who vowed never to forgive Aels or take a wife, hears of her death. It is a moment of poignant regret and self-questioning. Roberts's use of nature symbolism is effective – the long, hard freeze is clearly a reflection of the process of alienation that has afflicted Eban over the long years since his rejection, but at the same time the freezing weather is actual, felt, vividly recalled and not simply serving a symbolic purpose. The description of the domestic interior after the snowfall in the night is a small indication of this: 'Bore drannoeth goleuni dieithr yn y tŷ a'i deffroes. Yr oedd y tŷ yn dywyll ac yn olau ar yr un pryd' (Next morning it was a strange light in the house that awoke him. The house was dark and light at the same time).[34]

'Plant' (Children), like 'Dwy Storm', is set in the nineteenth century and again focuses on the north Welsh quarrying community from which Roberts's own family sprang. Indeed, this story appears to draw on an actual fragment of family history, one which is also mentioned in Roberts's autobiography, Y Lôn Wen, namely the death of a 12-year-old boy, Daniel, while working in the quarry. The story attempts to take the reader back into the midst of the lives of child workers of that time, both the little quarry lads like Daniel and the little girls who became maids of all work. The child's point of view is convincingly conveyed but the story is structurally flawed, and the ending somewhat anticlimactic.

'Y Taliad Olaf' (The Last Payment) focuses not on children but on a woman in old age, Ffani Rolant. Like Eban in 'Dwy Storm', she is an isolated figure: 'gyda hi ei hun y gallai hi ymgyfachrathu orau. Prin y gallai neb ddeall ei meddyliau, neb o'i chymdogion na'i gŵr hyd yn oed' (it was with herself alone that she was best able to communicate. No one could understand her thoughts, none of her neighbours and not even her husband).[35] This night is a momentous occasion for her: the night on which she is at last able to make 'the final payment' to the shopkeeper, after an entire lifetime of being in his debt. Only Ffani herself is aware of the significance of this evening in her life. Her husband is indifferent, the male shopkeeper equally so. She is an old woman, looking towards death, displaced in a new house without roots, without responsibilities, finally without debts. Emptiness echoes throughout the text. The road to the shop is, Ffani muses, her own biography:

fifty years of Friday payments. The emphasis is on futility, monotony – what was the point of it all? The last payment which is the final emblem of triumph over a lifetime of poverty is, ironically, anti-climactic. She hesitates to make the last payment because it seems to set a seal on that futility. All she gets in return for her final payment is an erasure – her name is wiped out of the shopkeeper's book. No longer possessing an account, she herself is no longer of any account. It is almost as if it is the debts which have kept her yoked to life, as if the shopkeeper's weekly inscriptions conferred an identity upon her. This ostensibly simple story is reverberant with a theme found repeatedly in Roberts's writing: the way in which economic pressures mould and in a sense *create* working-class female identity. Elsewhere she noted that she always got on well with her rival Communist campaigners when out canvassing for Plaid Genedlaethol Cymru in the Rhondda; her obsessive concern with the economic base perhaps suggests that she was on the same wavelength as them. And certainly Roberts's *oeuvre* would be fertile ground for a Marxist critic such as Lukács, who would surely approve of an aspect of Roberts's stories that a number of her Welsh critics and readers have condemned: its recurring focus on money. She herself admitted: 'Mae rhywun wedi deud amdana i mod i'n sôn gormod am arian yn y storïau yma. Nid dyna yn hollol ydi o, ond mae'n rhaid i chi gael arian i fyw, ac mi roedd o'n boen mawr iddyn nhw' (Someone has said about me that I have too much to say about money in these stories. That's not it exactly, but you have to have money to live, and it was a source of great suffering to them [the people of whom she writes]).[36]

'Y Taliad Olaf' is a magnificent story but, in Roberts's own opinion and in that of a number of critics, it is excelled by another story in the volume, 'Y Condemniedig'. Here, the condemned man of the title is Dafydd Pari, who has been told by his doctor that he is dying and that there is no cure for his illness. He returns home to his wife, Laura, and the story is a chronicle of the last months of his life at home. A quarryman unaccustomed to being idle, Dafydd learns in these final months the rhythms and patterns of the domestic world inhabited by his wife. For the first time, he realizes the extent and importance of her work, in the house and on the smallholding. It is a revelation to him. He comes to understand that they have been inhabiting separate spheres and is overwhelmed with regret that it has taken a fatal disease to make him understand and appreciate everything about his wife. As he lies on his sickbed, he begins to learn the 'language' of the house, its characteristic sounds and smells, which become comforting to him as he learns to interpret them and thus follow Laura's busy progress through her working day. He begins to notice details about Laura's appearance, too, which he has always in the past been too busy to take in: 'gwyddai 'rŵan, yr hyn na wyddai o'r blaen, faint o fotymau oedd ar ei bodis, beth oedd patrwm ei hances frethyn, sawl pleten oedd yn ei barclod' (he knew now, those things he didn't know before, how many buttons were on her bodice, what the pattern on her flannel handkerchief was, how many pleats her apron had).[37] Ironically enough, these last months are ones of intimacy and tenderness, though he finds himself still unable to articulate his love for Laura in words. The story is intensely and poignantly focalized upon Dafydd, giving no access to Laura's consciousness, but the reader sees from her behaviour, her care for Dafydd and her silent tears that she both knows very well what the doctor's verdict has been and that she returns Dafydd's unspoken love. This is a story that treads a very delicate line between despair and joy: Dafydd's feeling for Laura remains unspoken, and yet the story celebrates that mute love. On the one hand, the story presents a devastating portrayal of the way in which life carries on relentlessly while one man dies, but on the other hand that indefatigable persistence of life, the seasons, harvest, the round of domestic chores, is itself something positive.

In the years between the two world wars, then, Kate Roberts found her voice as a writer of short stories and a single novel later recognized as a classic. She used her apprenticeship in the drama to create stories with arresting, often epiphanic structures, and incorporating lively and authentic direct speech, using dialectal voices from both north and south Wales. At the same time, she drew on her very wide reading, both of Welsh-language texts ranging from the *Mabinogion* to the works of her contemporaries, such as Saunders Lewis and D. J. Williams, and of anglophone and world literature, extending from Joyce and Woolf to Chekhov and Mansfield, to shape and create the modern short story in Wales. She was fortunate in gaining the friendship of Saunders Lewis early on in her writing career; their extraordinary correspondence has left a record of the mutually sustaining relationship of these two gifted writers, who praise and critique each other's work and urge each other on to further literary experiment. But her relationship with Saunders Lewis also alerts us to another aspect of Roberts's life: the political aspect, for she and Lewis shared a passionate nationalist commitment. Both writers also had a mutual interest in gender politics, but Roberts's involvement is predicated on her life and experiences as a woman in a Wales which was still very much a man's world. These political interests are expressed most eloquently not in her fiction but in her journalism.

Roberts's political 'self-fashioning' takes place in her much-neglected non-fictional writing. Her work as a journalist and editor on *Baner ac Amserau Cymru* and *Y Ddraig Goch* offers an insight into her political beliefs and goals. The relationship between her political ideology and her writing comes to the foreground here, whereas in her fictional writing it is clear that she took pains to avoid slipping into political propaganda. Consideration of Roberts's complex and often conflicted politics – socialist, nationalist and feminist – will help to illuminate the reasons for her much-vaunted but misleading creative silence during the years between 1937 and 1949.

At the end of 1938, after protracted negotiations, Morris T. Williams and Kate Roberts succeeded in buying the important newspaper, *Baner ac Amserau Cymru* later known simply as *Y Faner* (The Banner) from the *Cambrian News*. From 1939 onwards it came under the aegis of Gee and Son in Denbigh and for the next decade would become the main forum for Kate Roberts's prolific journalism. This is the stage in her life which is traditionally regarded by critics as her silent period, since she published no volumes of fiction between 1937 and 1949. But this critical view is itself a silencing, since Kate Roberts's voice was in fact still to be heard loud and clear, largely speaking from the pages of *Y Faner*.

But her apprenticeship as a journalist had already been served long before she arrived in Denbigh. From September 1926 until November 1929, Roberts had been responsible for a section entitled 'Cylch y merched' (The women's circle) in *Y Ddraig Goch*, the official monthly magazine of the newly formed political party, Plaid Genedlaethol Cymru. In her first article in September 1926, she writes a very radical political essay about the aims of the new nationalist party, emphasizing the need for a wholesale change in the system of law and government, not just a commitment to the Welsh language and culture.[38] In the early numbers of *Y Ddraig Goch*, Roberts's articles focus on traditional crafts, customs, food and furniture; as she notes: 'Ein hamcan ni, bobl y Blaid Genedlaethol, yw cael popeth yn Gymreig' (Our aim, we people of the National Party, is for everything to be Welsh).[39]

Later articles tackle broader issues, such as education for girls (February, March and May 1927) in which she laments the focus on rote learning and passing exams and stresses the need for encouraging independence of mind in girl pupils. In fact, she condemns the over-production of female teachers in Wales and their inevitable migration to England for work; she suggests that Welsh women would be better off staying at home and thinking of following other career paths, such as architecture or hairdressing. She also remarks on the continuing prejudice in Wales against the education of girls, who are seen to 'waste' the money invested in them by getting married; in May 1927, not long before her own unexpected marriage, Roberts wrote:

Ond os oes unrhyw anturiaeth mewn bywyd y dylid cael addysg ar ei chyfair, priodi yw honno . . . [I'r hen bobl] dynes i gadw tŷ ac i fagu plant oedd gwraig. Ni wn a ydym wedi symud lawer ymlaen o'r fan yna yng Nghymru eto. Nid rhyfedd felly bod cymaint o ferched yn peidio â phriodi . . .[40]

(But if there is one adventure in life for which one requires an education, that adventure is marriage . . . [To the old folks] a wife was a woman who kept house and raised children. I don't know if we've moved on much from that attitude in Wales yet. It's no wonder, then, that so many women choose not to get married . . .)

Moreover, in June 1927, in outlining the advantages of a career in architecture for women, she notes 'Fel rheol, telir merched ar yr un raddfa a dynion (clywch clywch!)' (Normally, women (architects) are paid at the same rate as men (hear hear!)).[41]

In the 1928 Plaid Cymru summer school, Kate Roberts proposed a motion to convey to the Home Secretary and the Lord Chancellor members' indignation at the abusive remarks made by a London magistrate about the morality and probity of Welsh servant girls. Three such servants had been accused of stealing from the hotel where they were employed. Roberts's motion suggests, as Nia Williams has observed, her sense of solidarity with other women of her own class, who had not been fortunate enough to gain an education, as she herself had done.[42] Roberts's indignation may also have been connected with her strong feelings for her mother, a woman of considerable intellect, who had been sent away from home as a servant girl when she was barely ten years old. Her compassion for girls in such circumstances also finds fictional form in her stories about Laura Jones and about Winni Ffinni Hadog later in her career. These early journalistic articles on 'women's issues', then, reveal a confident, independent, politically aware female teacher keen on equal opportunities and equal pay. Pulling in a contrary direction is the passionate nationalist who is angry at witnessing the traditional Welsh way of life crumbling around her and desirous to hold on to and rebuild those traditions, some of which, surely, are likely to keep women in a traditionally secondary role and social position. In this early journalism, it is the voice of the first Kate Roberts that predominates but, later in life, when she returns to journalism as co-owner and editor of Y *Faner*, it is the second voice, the conservative voice of tradition which predominates, drowning out the younger feminist. Arguably, there is a third voice discernible in these early articles for *Y Ddraig Goch*, however, and that is the voice which perhaps concerns us later readers of Roberts's work most: the voice of the creative artist, the imaginative, transgressive and original voice of the writer of fiction.

In July 1927, *Y Ddraig Goch* carried one of her best-known short stories, 'Between Two Pieces of Toffee' (later republished, as we have noted, in the volume *Rhigolau Bywyd*). But in addition to publishing actual works of fiction such as this in the paper, Roberts sometimes introduced a strong dose of fiction into her journalistic articles, too. She was more than capable of mocking her fellow party members and subjecting them to ridicule in some of her fictional flights of fancy. In the August 1928 issue, for example, she imagines a great bazaar held to raise funds for the party and takes some pleasure in placing her illustrious male peers in quasi-female roles at the bazaar's various stands, such as: 'Stondin Fwyta. Yn gwasanaethu wrth y byrddau fydd Caradog Pritchard, W. J. Roberts (Bangor), Tom Parri, E. Prosser Rhys. Edrychent yn bur ddel mewn capiau a ffedogau gwynion' (Food Stall. Serving at the tables will be Caradog Pritchard, W. J. Roberts (Bangor), Tom Parri, E. Prosser Rhys. They look quite pretty in their white caps and aprons).[43] Slyly, she places herself and her friend Tegwen Clee in charge of the wine stall! The most outrageous of these fictional flights of fancy in *Y Ddraig Goch*, though, came in July 1929 where she imagines the annual Plaid summer school in the year 1976: in this future Wales, Saunders Lewis is the Welsh prime minister, R. Williams Parry the national poet, Lewis Valentine MP for Caernarfon, Tegwen Clee MP for Llanelli, Cassie Davies education minister, all in the new Welsh senate in mid-Wales (this fantasy is reminiscent, too, of her very first published story, 'Y Diafol yn 1960', though the tone here is much more light-hearted). In this utopian vision of the future, where all her friends from the 'BB' are given a role, there are a few notable gaps, including the author herself; tongue-in-cheek, she notes that Kate Roberts has died of a broken heart because no one was willing to write for the women's column of *Y Ddraig Goch*![44]

From this point until the mid-1930s, Roberts's contributions to the party's official journal become less and less frequent, and by the later 1930s they have more or less ceased. In retrospect, what is striking about her early journalism is its remarkable willingness to be plain-spoken. Roberts can be a cutting critic, especially of her own people, the Welsh, in much the same way as the poet R. S. Thomas was to become in the latter half of the century. In these early articles, for example, she bewails Welsh people's willingness to forget their own language and customs in their eagerness to be Anglicized; she asks rhetorically in August 1927, 'A fu erioed genedl o lyngyrrod mor ddiasgwrn-cefn â ni'r Cymry?' (Was there ever such a nation of spineless worms as us Welsh?).[45] Similarly, in February 1931, she hacks the novelist E. Tegla Davies's literary reputation to shreds, claiming that he began with great promise and has gone downhill ever since. His problem, she alleges, is that he never criticizes his own work rigorously enough to be able to develop as a writer. In the small world of Welsh-language letters, such a lengthy negative review – accurate and penetrating as it certainly is – was not calculated to win Kate Roberts many friends. However cruel, it shows clearly where her priorities always lay: to tell the truth, no matter what the consequences.

The later journalism, contained in the pages of *Baner ac Amserau Cymru* (later simply *Y Faner*) shares some of the same features as the *Y Ddraig Goch* writing, and there is certainly a continuity of voice. Nevertheless, there is a noticeable shift away from the radical opinions of the sparky young feminist towards a more entrenched, and possibly embittered, traditionalism. In the issue of *Baner ac Amserau Cymru* dated 30 June 1948, for example, under the title 'Arian yw duw Cymru' (Money is the god of Wales), we can read the text of Roberts's speech as she chaired a local Eisteddfod in Llangwm.[46] It is a typically mordant attack on Welsh people's willingness to sell their inheritance for a mess of pottage. As the title suggests, it is cutting about the chapel hierarchy and its hypocrisy. Alluding to Samuel Butler, it echoes his remark about how astonished everyone would be in our society if someone actually began to live as a Christian. In the same issue of the paper, though, is an essay by Roberts entitled 'Y ferch fodern' (The modern woman), which is in essence a celebration of the achievements of women since the Victorian age.[47] She emphasizes the disadvantages women of all classes suffered in the past, giving particular attention to the practical difficulties and downright pain of Victorian women's clothing. She gives special emphasis to the achievements of women writers in the twentieth century. The second half of the column is dedicated to a contemporary woman architect, Cynthia Wood, who has learned Welsh and is building good cottages for Welsh rural workers. Here, then, we see strong echoes of the feminist Kate Roberts willing to challenge the old hegemony of the chapel and to champion the accomplishments of women. Yet, in these issues of *Y Faner* from the 1940s, Roberts once again finds herself in charge of the women's column, much as she had been, to her evident frustration, in *Y Ddraig Goch* in the 1920s, and we thus find her giving advice on housework and providing useful recipes. This occurs while, on another page of the newspaper, Saunders Lewis holds forth in his famous column, 'Cwrs y byd' (The way of the world), writing authoritatively on world events. Despite Roberts's celebration of women's liberation, the pages of her own newspaper demonstrate how the chains of gender are still firmly hobbling women's feet.

In the 12 December 1956 issue of *Baner ac Amserau Cymru*, amid intense discussion of the struggle to save Tryweryn from drowning, Kate Roberts provides an essay entitled 'Merched mewn swyddi uchel' (Women in high office).[48] This is an astute analysis of the phenomenon which later came to be known as the glass ceiling. It is almost as if Roberts herself is revisiting her article of eight years previously in which she celebrated women's achievements and is now asking why aren't there more women in the top jobs? She points out that there are very few women professors, almost no senior consultants in hospitals who are women and less than a handful of women in the cabinet at Westminster (with regard to the latter point, fifty-four years later, nothing has changed, indicating the enduring strength of the patriarchal structures that

Roberts so astutely recognized). She suggests that the reasons for women's lack of success in high office is not related to their ability; rather, it can be attributed to the conservatism of both men and women in a society which is not yet convinced that women are capable of leadership. Roberts points out the uncomfortable fact that women still seem to be saddled with the hardest and the least well-paid jobs, such as nursing and housework. She has noticed too in her travels around the country that it is the women who are most active in chapels and other local societies and events: 'Ymddengys i mi mai'r dynion sy'n penderfynu penderfyniadau, ac mai'r merched sydd yn gweithio. Na chymerwn ein twyllo gan ambell ddyrchafiad i ferch, mewn sefyllfa is-raddol y mae'r ferch o hyd' (It seems to me that it's men who make the decisions, and it is women who do the work. Let's not let ourselves be misled by the occasional woman reaching high office, women are still in a subordinate position).[49] She points out to those who would argue that women do not have the experience to govern that it would be very hard for any woman to make such a mess of governing as the present male incumbents at Westminster. Roberts was clear-sighted, then, about women's position in society.

However, in the permissive 1960s, even in a Wales that was arguably more resistant to the sexual and other freedoms it heralded, Kate Roberts, by now in her seventies, gradually moved away from the unmistakably feminist ideology she had hitherto embraced in her journalism. As Francesca Rhydderch notes in her essay 'They do not breed de Beauvoirs here', 'an interesting disjunction emerges during the 1960s in Roberts' work, between her increasingly conservative journalism on women on the one hand, and the quite radical and probing interior monologue of the novels and novellas which she wrote between 1949 and 1969.'[50] It is as if the two Kate Robertses, who have always been present in her writing, at this point become definitively split.

Virginia Woolf referred to the spectre of the 'angel in the house' whom every woman writer had to struggle against and attempt to kill, because she would prevent her writing.[51] Roberts was very much aware of this spectre, chafed against her for years but, eventually, allowed her to guide her pen in her later journalism. In comparison to Woolf and to Simone de Beauvoir, both of whose work Roberts knew and admired, Roberts had a more problematic relation to feminism as an ideology. Partly, at least, this is a consequence of being a member of a minority-language grouping and an embattled culture, whereas both Woolf and Beauvoir had the privilege of belonging to imperial cultures of international prestige. Thus, Roberts had a very different relation to tradition than did her feminist peers from England and France; she also found herself in a literary culture in which she was for years virtually the only woman, known always in Welsh as 'brenhines ein llên' (the queen of our literature), emphasizing her singularity and isolation. That she herself did not welcome this role is evident in her early collaboration with other women writers; she seemed to want to belong to a community of women authors (as her correspondence with women such as Storm Jameson, Margiad Evans, Lilla Wagner, Vera Brittain and others indicates) but she found herself largely in the company of men. And, in such company, she always found herself reluctantly in charge of the 'women's column'.

Kate Roberts was a twentieth-century writer but, like her contemporary, Virginia Woolf, she was brought up in the Victorian age, with its more rigid ideology of gender. It is of course important to remember that Welsh Victorian gender discourses differed significantly from those of England, as a number of feminist critics, such as Jane Aaron and Ceridwen Lloyd-Morgan, have pointed out.[52] Certainly, the passive and physically delicate model of the angel in the house which was espoused in Victorian England and propagated by writers such as Dickens was never the dominant ideal in Victorian Wales, where even domestic angels were expected to be relatively robust and perennially busy. The maternal ideal has been extremely important in the Welsh ideology of femininity in a way which surpasses even its prominence in England, perhaps because, as Rhydderch notes, Welsh motherhood is seen as a 'cultural motherhood' as well as a physical, moral and familial role.[53] In other words, the Welsh mam nurtures a whole community, a language, history, memory and culture, enshrining and elevating her role even higher than her English counterpart. In-creasingly, Kate Roberts found herself as a journalist and public figure inhabiting this cultural mother role, ironically enough, in view of her own childlessness. The iconography of Kate Roberts in late twentieth-century Wales moreover supported this image: only photographs of the elderly, grandmotherly Kate Roberts ever seemed to be used in the press, erasing the younger woman from the national consciousness. This volume attempts to resurrect that expunged and essential figure.

4

'The struggle of a woman's soul': 1946–1960

Although, true to his political beliefs, Morris T. Williams in 1940 registered as a conscientious objector, the Second World War and its immediate aftermath would be a time of bereavement and loss for Kate Roberts, as the previous war had been. In 1944, her mother died; in 1945, E. Prosser Rhys died. During 1945, Morris T. Williams was involved in a rather bitter exchange of letters with Rhys's widow, Prudence. Williams had assumed that he would be offered Rhys's press, Gwasg Aberystwyth, as a matter of course, but his widow put it on the market instead, understandably concerned for her own and her daughter's future financial security. Having resolved this misunderstanding, though, life did not progress smoothly for Kate Roberts and her husband. In 1946, Morris T. Williams, still a young man, died suddenly.[1] In an interview with her friend, Lewis Valentine, published in 1963, Roberts said that in 1946 'syrthiodd fy myd yn deilchion o'm cwmpas. Y pryd hynny y dechreuais edrych i mewn i mi fy hun, a'r canlyniad cyntaf oedd *Stryd y Glep*, lle y disgrifir ymdrech enaid dynes' (my world fell to pieces around me. It was then that I started to look into my own mind, and the first result was *Gossip Row*, which describes the struggle of a woman's soul).[2] The shock and grief of her sudden bereavement was deeply felt and long-lasting; even in 1982, Roberts could write in her journal: '36 mlynedd i heddiw y bu Morris farw. Ymddengys fel ddoe' (thirty-six years ago today Morris died. It seems like yesterday).[3] Even if the marriage had not been as happy as she must have hoped, since it was overshadowed towards the end by her husband's worsening alcoholism, his loss was an overwhelming blow for her. They were, after all, a childless couple who had lived for the past twenty years not only as husband and wife but as partners in an exhausting business, as fellow political campaigners and as writers who frequently collaborated on journalistic pieces and who carefully read each other's work. They therefore were in each other's company far more often than the conventional married couple of the day, where the husband would be out of the house earning a wage, and the wife would stay at home taking care of the domestic space (as represented so poignantly in Roberts's story, 'Y Condemniedig'). Now, at the age of fifty-five, Kate Roberts was left alone, a widow, struggling with a loss-making business, mounting debts, frustration at the lack of opportunity to do her own writing and an appalling weight of grief over the husband who had been taken away from her at such an early age. It must have seemed to her that her life was a catalogue of loss and suffering, the bereavement of 1946 echoing what she had felt almost thirty years before at the loss of her brother, David, during the First World War.

Interestingly, Roberts's response to this second, devastating bereavement was the same as the one she had made, self-defensively, to the first; namely, to write. In a radio broadcast, Roberts stated: 'Nid tywyllu fy meddwl wnaeth fy mhrofedigaeth [o golli ei gŵr] ond agor drysau ar Fywyd, a gweld pethau a phobl yn gliriach. Ond yn lle edrych yn ôl ar y gorffennol, dechreuais edrych i mewn i fi fy hun ac ar fy mhrofiadau' (My bereavement [when her husband died] did not darken my mind so much as open up new doors upon Life, [allowing me] to see things and people more clearly. But instead of looking back at the past, I began to look inward, inside myself and my experiences).[4]

The texts from this period reveal a Kate Roberts now ready to experiment much more boldly with form and voice, though her concern with gender, economics and human relationships remains constant. In the 1950s, Roberts published two novels, namely *Y Byw sy'n Cysgu* (The Living Sleep; 1956) and *Tegwch y Bore* (Fairness of Morning; 1957–8). The former takes her away from her usual realist mode into lengthy passages of dream and interior monologue; she also incorporates extracts from the female protagonist's journal. While the novel tackles contemporary concerns about marital and social breakdown, it is also very much an exploration of a woman attempting to gain an autonomous identity through a therapeutic act of writing. One can see, therefore, that the exploration of the psyche of a woman who has experienced the loss of a husband can be linked directly to her own post-war experience, while the second novel, *Tegwch y Bore*, takes her right back to the pre-First World War era when she was still in the midst of that stage of youth in which one is almost unaware of one's own happiness. One of Roberts's best-known works, *Te yn y Grug* (Tea in the Heather; 1959), also belongs to this period; it ranges even further back into the experiences of childhood and early adolescence, and reveals how she productively blurs the generic boundaries between adult and children's fiction.

Saunders Lewis responded to the first of Roberts's works of this period, *Stryd y Glep*, with great enthusiasm, calling it in a letter of 27 April 1949 'a masterpiece', far better than any of her previous stories, and comparing it to some of the short fiction of André Gide. 'O'r diwedd', he says, 'dyma ddyfnder seicolegol ac aeddfedrwydd nofelydd mawr yn y Gymraeg' (At last we have in Welsh a fiction of psychological depth which reflects the maturity of a great novelist).[5] Aneirin Talfan Davies, the radio producer and critic, also wrote to Roberts in praise of her new work, which he calls 'a little classic of fine writing, uncommon vision, and deep penetration into the hidden places of the human heart'. Interestingly, he too reaches for French texts with which to compare Roberts, citing François Mauriac's 'The Woman of the Pharisees' as a similar work.[6]

Stryd y Glep takes the form of a first-person narrative by the disabled protagonist, Ffebi Beca, who writes in her diary. The action of the text extends from May to September in a year when Ffebi's hitherto monotonous life changes dramatically. The form is given on the title page as a 'stori fer hir ar ffurf dyddiadur' (a long short story in the form of a diary), a cumbersome description of which Saunders Lewis is dismissive, calling it instead, in the French style, a 'nouvelle'. This is a highly inward-looking narrative, focusing exclusively on the thoughts, feelings and observations of Ffebi (Phoebe). Her invalid status means that she is unable to move from her bed, unless carried outside by her brother and neighbour. Her paralysis (as the result of an accidental fall while working in the family shop) has lasted three years and it is clear that Roberts is using Ffebi's condition as a metaphor for the stagnant, monotonous and incestuous condition of the society of this small and small-minded north Welsh town, much as James Joyce used the recurrent image of paralysis in the stories of *Dubliners*. The narrative offers an unflattering portrait of Welsh life, centred on chapel and shop, with the main concern of its inhabitants seemingly being to gossip and make snide remarks about neighbours. Families are seen as a source of anxiety and a form of prison. And yet there are positive aspects to this society, too – there is lifelong friendship here, considerable kindness and a real bond between sisters. Middle-aged women are seen as being at the mercy of men, who wield the economic power in society; unmarried middle-aged women are seen as scheming, competitive and even mentally unbalanced. The portrayal of Miss Jones, house-keeper to Dan Meidrym, is of a woman on the edge of a mental breakdown.

Although the text is not autobiographical in a straightforward sense, it is interesting to note that the narrative begins with a death (that of Rhys Glanmor), which is the subject of much gossip and speculation, possibly reflecting Roberts's own recent experience of the sudden death of her husband. As Ffebi reflects in her diary:

Mae'n rhyfedd fel y stwffia'r byw ar ôl y marw, mynd ar ei ôl cyn belled ag y medrant, tynnu ei enaid allan ohono a'i roi yn ôl wedyn, mynd i'w bocedi a'u gwagio a rhoi eu cynnwys yn ôl wedyn, ac wedi gwneud hynny, gadael llonydd iddo fo, a dechrau ar ei deulu . . .[7]

(It's strange how the living pursue the dead, following them as far as they can, extracting the soul from the dead person and then replacing it, searching his pockets and emptying them and then putting their contents back, and after doing all that, leaving him alone, and starting on his family . . .)

The narrative is full of satirical digs at a hypocritical chapel-going society; Ffebi's circle of friends in Gossip Row like nothing better than to comment on the Sunday sermon, usually negatively, though as Ffebi tartly observes, 'Fe gewch bawb, hyd yn oed gybyddion, i gytuno fod pregeth yn erbyn ariangarwch yn un dda' (You'll get everyone, even misers, to agree that a sermon against monetary greed is a good one).[8] By the end of the narrative, Ffebi feels guilt and remorse for her feelings of hatred and jealousy, which have been fostered by Gossip Row, and has a moment of insight in which she is able to acknowledge her own selfishness and self-deception. The diary ends with a quotation from a fifteenth-century *cywydd* by Siôn Cent: 'Gobeithiaw a ddaw ydd wyf' (My hope lies in what is to come).[9] The poem refers to the future of Wales and has been seen as referring to the 'mab darogan' (son of prophecy) who will save the country, but Ffebi hopes for a personal, spiritual and perhaps even physical resurrection.

Ffebi is not a particularly likeable character and the community of Gossip Row is a particularly acid representation of traditional Welsh society. Nevertheless, it rings true. Ffebi's immersion in her own thoughts and in the narrow confines of her world can be seen as a fictional projection of Roberts's own experience of bereavement and depression, the hope glimpsed at the end of the story perhaps an indication of its author's emergence from the despondent self-absorption of the bereaved. It is unsurprising to find Saunders Lewis being particularly appreciative of this short text, since it is reminiscent of his own, equally negative, representation of Welsh suburban life in his 1930 novel, *Monica*. Roberts had written to Lewis on 12 January 1931 to express her admiration of his controversial novel, noting 'mae eich disgrifiadau o'r Dre newydd a'i phobl yn odidog. Yn wir fe aeth ias o ofn drwof wrth feddwl mai un o'r bobl yna wyf i, yn cadw'r caead, efallai, ar grochan berw' (your description of the new Town and its people is excellent. In truth a shudder of fear went through me as I thought that I am one of those people, keeping the lid, perhaps, on a boiling cauldron).[10] Though at the time Roberts was living in the new 'garden village' of Rhiwbina in northern Cardiff, she proved herself equally capable of drawing an unflattering fictional picture of the old town of Denbigh and the repressed and gnawing passions of characters living there almost twenty years later.

Also in 1946, there appeared the first selection of English translations of Roberts's short stories, in the form of the volume entitled *A Summer Day and Other Stories*. Published by the Penmark Press in Cardiff, it featured an enthusiastic introduction by the English writer, Storm Jameson, who was then an admired and influential literary figure. The intention of the volume was clearly to introduce the work of Kate Roberts to an anglophone audience, and it set about doing so in an authoritative manner. As the dust-jacket of the original edition declares: 'Kate Roberts is one of the best short story writers of our day . . . she is the most distinguished craftsman in the Welsh language, and those English critics who have commented on her few translated stories are emphatic that her place is with the great European masters of this difficult form.'[11] That the volume was read by at least some of the leading writers of the day is suggested by the fact that H.D.'s (the Modernist poet, Hilda Doolittle) autographed copy of the book is today housed with her papers in the Beinecke Rare Books Library in Yale.[12]

The volume contains twelve stories, as follows: 'Two Storms' (trans. Dafydd Jenkins); 'The Wind' (trans. Dafydd Jenkins); 'The Loss' (trans. Walter Dowding); 'The Quilt' (trans. Wyn Griffith); 'Old Age' (trans. Wyn Griffith); 'A Summer Day' (trans. Dafydd Jenkins); 'Between Two Pieces of Toffee' (trans. Walter Dowding); 'The Letter' (trans. Wyn Griffith); 'Final Payment' (trans. Wyn Griffith); 'Sisters' (trans. Walter Dowding); 'The Condemned' (trans. Dafydd Jenkins); 'Folded Hands' (trans. Wyn Griffith). A number of these stories had already appeared in the Faber and Penguin collections of *Welsh Short Stories*, in *Life and Letters Today* and in *The Welsh Review*, suggesting that Roberts's work was already gaining a reputation both in Wales and England at the time.

Storm Jameson in introducing the volume takes up the position of mediator: she presents herself as a writer from the north of

England who has lived in Wales for two and a half years, con-ceding that 'Wales is easy to reach and not easy to know'.[13] She professes 'ignorant love' for a country with what she calls a 'living culture which is not that of the elsewhere triumphant machine age'. Determinedly placing Roberts in a European context, she compares Wales to Slovakia, since both are small countries with 'a native culture which has so much energy left'.[14] Turning specific-ally to Kate Roberts, Jameson admires her

> observation [which] is direct and brilliantly convincing. She offers only the significant detail . . . In the sharp clarity of her descriptive writing . . . not only the thing seen, but things heard, touched, tasted, are evoked with an energy and purity which succeed because they are loyal first of all to the thing itself: the emotion springs from it, is not merely thrown round it.[15]

She goes so far as to compare Roberts to Chekhov, as well as to contemporary English story-writers, such as H. E. Bates and V. S. Pritchett, preferring the Welsh writer's work because it is, she says, 'enriched and steadied by her deep sense of continuity with the past . . . This buried and yet active sense . . . of a complex tradition.'[16]

In the 1950s, Kate Roberts attempted to rekindle her earlier interest in writing drama. By this period there were new opportun-ities in radio and, within the next decade, television, which could offer not only a creative forum for her work but also some much-needed income. Roberts's papers in the National Library of Wales contain a number of unpublished manuscripts of radio dramas from this period, including *Y Cynddrws* (The Lobby), which was broadcast on 25 May 1954 (directed by Aneirin Talfan Davies). This is an absurdist drama revolving around a group of characters in a waiting room; it soon becomes evident that they are all dead and awaiting the summons to proceed elsewhere. Some of the characters are historical figures, such as the eighteenth-century poet, Goronwy Owen, while others appear to be more allegorical or representative – a widow who has lost two sons in the war, a tramp and a rich farmer. The drama strikes the reader as distinctly absurdist and Beckettian, though it is as well to remember that the English version of *Waiting for Godot* did not premiere in London until several years later. The play also draws on the Welsh 'anterliwt' (interlude) tradition, appropriately enough, since the main character is an eighteenth-century poet. The play's setting is clearly not intended to be realistic but the behaviour of the characters is all too recognizable, their bickering and comic repartee being somewhat reminiscent of the action of Roberts's earliest co-authored comedies from thirty years before. In Beckettian fashion *avant la lettre* nothing much happens but, at the end, Sion the tramp unexpectedly gets let through the door to the life beyond first, leaving the others indignant and complaining loudly. Although the play is open to a number of interpretations, it may be seen to echo the author's view, as expressed in her address at Llangwm Eisteddfod in 1948 (mentioned above) that despite Wales's appearance of being a Christian country, if anyone actually lived by Christian principles in contemporary Wales, he would be shunned and ridiculed. Perhaps the tramp, Sion, penniless, homeless and unrespectable, is the nearest Roberts could come at the time to imagining a character who might be allowed into the kingdom of heaven.

Another drama from this period is *Modryb a Nith* (Aunt and Niece), which exists both as a prose narrative and as a four-part radio drama among Roberts's papers.[17] The drama was broadcast on Radio Cymru in May 1959 from Neuadd y Penrhyn, with Wilbert Lloyd Roberts directing. The contrast in this drama is between Sera Huws, who is deeply in mourning over the death of her sister, whom she has spent years looking after, and her niece, Let Huws, who is full of youthful joy over her recent engagement. This juxtaposition is clearly one which appealed to the author, since she reworked it several times, perhaps because it stands as an emblem of human loneliness, the impossibility of knowing another person or truly understanding another's experience. Indeed, as the elderly shopkeeper in Roberts's late story 'Cwsmeriaid' (Customers; from *Yr Wylan Deg* (The Fair Seagull), 1976) reflects: 'oes posibl dwad i adnabod pobl o gwbl?' (is it possible to know people at all?).[18] One might argue that the whole fictional enterprise, that imaginative entry into other people's lives and feelings, is a kind of substitute for the impossibility of this process in our everyday lives. People often found Kate Roberts quite a formidable, reticent and rather prickly character; she herself sometimes spoke of her loneliness, especially in old age. The richness, scope and variety of her fiction, therefore, and its astonishingly empathetic quality, may be seen as a sublimation of emotions and desires for intimacy which were denied her in life. In the radio drama, *Modryb a Nith*, the situations of the two protagonists are completely changed around by the end: Let has broken off her engagement and determined to be a modern, independent woman, while her aunt Sera has overcome her grief and accepted the marriage proposal of her old friend, Sam. The drama focuses intensely on the empathy between these two women and the choices that women face in their lives. Unlike the rather sombre tone of much of Roberts's fiction of this period and later, however, she is able to draw here on her early apprenticeship as a comic dramatist, successfully creating a drama of voices which addresses important issues and is yet leavened with humour and light-hearted banter, as well as a good-humoured satire of small-town parochialism.

Another interesting drama manuscript from the period is one entitled *Y Gwas* (The Servant), which is accompanied by a number of letters (dated 1960 and 1961) from Emyr Humphreys at the BBC, giving Roberts advice on suggested changes to the script before broadcast. Unlike the fantastical and absurdist *Y Cynddrws* and the more genial and comic *Modryb a Nith*, *Y Gwas* is an historical drama that draws on some of Roberts's earlier writings about Caernarfonshire in the nineteenth century. The play turns around the courtship of Gwen, daughter of Hendre Fawr farm and Huw, who comes to the farm as a servant boy. The play focuses on change – the breaching of class barriers in the marriage of Gwen and Huw, the beginning of the slate quarries and of the decline in the fortunes of the landed gentry. Huw is imprisoned for allegedly burning the Lord Penllyn's hayricks but he eventually emerges from jail and starts work in the new quarry. The final scene is highly reminiscent of the end of Zola's great nineteenth-century novel, *Germinal*: Gwen reflects self-consciously as she goes out onto the mountainside with Huw: 'Ella'n bod ni yma heno yn mynd trwy wewyr esgor rhyw fyd newydd fydd i ddwad i bawb, wrth gwffio yn erbyn yr hen fyd' (Perhaps here tonight we are going through the pains of giving birth to a new future world for everyone, as we struggle against the old world). Unsurprisingly, Humphreys had his work cut out as a producer to try to make this sprawling narrative into a work for radio; arguably, his efforts were not enough to make this into a successful drama.

But Roberts had not turned her back on fiction. Her novel *Y Byw sy'n Cysgu* (The Living Sleep) was published in 1956; it was also broadcast on radio that year in a production by Emyr Humphreys. Roberts's extant correspondence shows that reception of this novel among her acquaintances was very positive. Enid Parry wrote to her on 4 January 1957, for instance, saying that she had abandoned her housework in order to finish the story of Lora Ffennig, adding that she thought Roberts had succeeded in penetrating the complexities of a woman's character better than any male novelist. D. J. Williams and Saunders Lewis were also enthusiastic about the work. Alun Llywelyn-Williams went even further and referred to the novel in a letter of 18 January 1957 as the best work she had ever written.

The contrast between *Y Byw sy'n Cysgu* and Roberts's previous full-length novel, *Traed mewn Cyffion*, could hardly be more marked. While the earlier novel is panoramic in scope, this novel is intensely introspective and, as a consequence, rather static. It intersperses third-person narration focalized on the central character, Lora Ffennig, with the first-person narration of Lora's own diary. Roberts had experimented successfully with the diary format in the earlier novella, *Stryd y Glep*, but here the text is more polyvocal, with Lora's inner voice being constantly juxtaposed with the thoughts and direct speech of other characters. Lora is a married woman with two children, whose husband has left her for another woman. The novel concerns her attempt to come to terms with this abandonment and to decide which direction to take in her future life. Clearly, the novel is not straightforwardly autobiographical, but it may be seen as an exploration of Roberts's own feelings after her bereavement, when she was also 'left' by her husband; at any rate, the penetration into Lora's inner world strikes the reader as authentic and convincing. Lora begins to depend on the journal that she writes, looking forward to pouring out her feelings into her book. Indeed, Lora sees this therapeutic act of writing as an effort at self-knowledge: 'mynd i gyfarfod a hi ei hun' (going to meet her own self).[19] For Lora is deeply repressed by her upbringing and her moral values; she knows that she would take her husband back if he were to return, not because she loves him but in order to appear respectable. Another man, Aleth Meurig, wishes to marry Lora, but she refuses to seek a divorce through the courts; as Aleth reflects,

> Pobl o'r wlad oeddynt o hyd, a Chymry at hynny, ac yr oedd pobl Cymru yn methu mwynhau eu pleserau am fod arnynt ofn peidio â bod yn dduwiol, ac yn methu mwynhau eu duwioldeb am fod arnynt eisiau dilyn eu chwantau.[20]

> (They were still country people, and Welsh people to boot, and the people of Wales were unable to enjoy their pleasures because they were afraid of not being pious, and they were unable to enjoy their piety because they wanted to pursue their desires).

Little is resolved in the workings of the plot: Iolo does not return, Lora does not marry again, but there is a sense in which Lora has found an awakening at last from her 'living sleep'.

Roberts's next novel, *Tegwch y Bore*, was first published in instalments in *Y Faner* between April 1957 and April 1958. It was not published as a separate volume until 1967, because she was unsure of its literary worth, but was persuaded by friends eventually to publish it. It is clearly a highly autobiographical novel, set between 1913 and 1917, years of the author's life which remain largely un-narrated in her 1960 autobiography, *Y Lôn Wen*. It is interesting to surmise why this crucial portion of her life had to be turned into fiction, rather than narrated in a more overtly autobiographical mode. Arguably, transforming these most intense of remembered experiences into fictional form allowed her to endow them with a happy ending. Indeed, it is this relatively happy ending which is, artistically, the least successful section of the novel as a whole. It is as if Roberts lapses into the clichés of romance in order to fit such an ending onto a novel that has been largely about loss, disappointment and grief.

It is also in this novel, through the fictionalized experience of her protagonist, Ann Owen, that Roberts sets out most clearly her own strong feelings for her youngest brother (named Bobi in the fiction – the diminutive form of the name is itself telling) and her devastation at his death during the war, many hundreds of miles away from home. The configuration of the Owen family is identical to that of the Robertses in Cae'r Gors: a hard-working quarryman father, a redoubtable Mam who keeps house and runs the smallholding, Ann herself the eldest and the only daughter, with three younger brothers. Ann's experience also matches her author's in that we first meet her as she graduates in Welsh from the university in Bangor, gets her first job in a local primary school and then has to move away from home to south Wales to obtain her first secondary school post. The loss of her youngest brother and the circumstances of his death are identical to those of Roberts herself, as is the serious injury to another brother. More problematic is the relationship between Ann and her lover, Richard Edmund, which appears to be based on Roberts's relationship with David Ellis, who had been a fellow student at Bangor and subsequently a soldier in the war. If this is the case, Roberts manipulates the facts of this relationship in order to effect a happy ending, whereas in fact David Ellis, like Roberts's little brother, Dei, died during the war. Perhaps Roberts was aware that her novel was becoming too Hardy-esque (Hardy himself is mentioned on several occasions in the novel, and Ann enjoys reading his works) in its unremitting sadness and the cruel twists of fate that prevent the characters from achieving a promised escape from poverty or conjugal happiness. In any case, the end of the novel sees Ann and Richard united with a hope of an early marriage and a suggestion that Richard's life is no longer in danger since he will not be sent out to France again. Such rewriting of real life must surely have had a therapeutic effect on the author but the artistic effect is not wholly successful, particularly in comparison with the early chapters of the novel, which are vividly narrated and radiate a sense of authenticity.

If Kate Roberts herself seems oddly absent from the centre of her autobiography, *Y Lôn Wen*, perhaps the closest we as readers can approach her is through her character, Ann Owen, in *Tegwch y Bore*. Unlike *Traed mewn Cyffion*, where there is no character who closely resembles the author herself, the details of Ann's biography are, as mentioned, very closely modelled on those of her creator, so it is perhaps not illegitimate of us to surmise that many of Ann's experiences, feelings and beliefs may also be those of Kate Roberts, at least as a young woman. Saunders Lewis commented on this when he wrote to her on Christmas Day 1967, having read the newly published edition of *Tegwch y Bore* which she had sent to him:

> Mae llawer iawn o'ch bywyd chi yn y nofel, ac mi fydd hi byw ac yn bwysig oherwydd hynny. Mae'r darlun o'r cefndir cyn y rhyfel yn werthfawr yr un modd, ac yn hanesol bwysig. Ond yr hyn sy'n greadigol bwysig yw'r astudiaeth o ofid a chariad Ann, a'r frwydr rhwng Bobi a Richard yn ei meddwl a'i chalon hi, rhwng y gorffennol a'r dyfodol, y teulu oedd a'r teulu a fyddai.[21]

> (There is a great deal of your own life in the novel, and it will live and be important because of that. The depiction of the background before the war is valuable in the same way, and is historically important. But what is *creatively* important is the study of Ann's worry and love, and the battle between Bobi and Richard in her mind and heart, between the past and the future, the family that was and the family that would be.)

As usual, Saunders Lewis's critique of the work is perceptive. The first half of the novel represents 'the family that was' and Ann's growing discontent with the duty she owes it for the 'privilege' of her education, as well as with the narrow-minded milieu of Blaen Ddôl society. Foreshadowing the imagery she would later use to describe Bet's depression in the novella, *Tywyll Heno*, she describes the place as 'fel rhyw fwgwd ar wyneb rhywun; mae'r byd yn symud yn i flaen ond 'dydi Blaen Ddôl ddim' (like some mask over one's face; the world moves on but Blaen Ddôl stays the same).[22] Ann embarks on her faltering relationship with Richard, but she has to come to terms with her problematic relations with other women, too: her mother is unappreciative of her achievements, while her landlady, Mrs Ifans, the kind of person for whom the correct positioning of doileys on plates is a matter of some importance, exasperates her. She maintains a correspondence with a college friend, Dora, which helps her express her growing frustration, and her close friendship with the unconventional Mrs Huws, wife of the chapel minister, sustains her further. But Ann finds another release from the drudgery of her teaching post through writing a play for the children in the chapel to perform; this is a recurring device in Roberts's work and is clearly a fictional representation of her own 'birth' as a writer. Ann finds herself beginning to look at people and situations in a different light once she begins to write creatively:

> dechreuai bwyso a mesur pethau a phobol, eu gosod yn eu lle mewn bywyd. Gwelai hwynt, nid fel bodau yn byw o ddydd i ddydd, yn ddiystyr, ond fel pethau â rhywbeth yn eu gwthio o'r tu ôl, a rhywbeth yn disgwyl amdanynt o'r tu blaen, ac yn barod i ddisgyn arnynt . . .[23]

> (she began to weigh and measure things and people, to put them in their place in life. She saw them, not as beings who lived from day to day, meaninglessly, but as things being pushed from behind, with something lying in wait in front of them, ready to fall upon them . . .)

In the second half of the novel, Ann has moved to a better teaching post in south Wales but her life is shadowed by the war – both Richard and Bobi have joined up and she is anxious about both, though Bobi's youth and innocence has the stronger pull on her. As she acknowledges herself, 'yr oedd arni hi eisiau iddo fod yn hogyn o hyd, yn hogyn trowsus pen glin' (she wanted him to remain a boy, a boy in short trousers).[24] When Bobi dies, she is overcome with grief and, for some time, cannot feel anything at all for Richard, who survives. Looking back on her life so far, she sees it as a meadow, one half bathed in the 'fair' light of 'morning', separated from the other half by a deep trench, which represents the war. Nevertheless, in the hopeful ending, Ann asserts a sense of continuity with the past and feels drawn once more to Richard because he, too, is associated with that pre-war world which was, in retrospect, so pristine.

Writing this highly autobiographical novel had taken Roberts right back to the first war, but the post-Second World War period had also been, for her as for many people, a time of austerity. She was well aware, though, that her own difficulty with making ends meet was as nothing compared with the extreme poverty and deprivation in many parts of post-war Europe. Indeed, as she had done during the Depression in the Rhondda, Roberts was active in her efforts to try to relieve this suffering, sending food and clothing parcels abroad via the Save Europe Now fund, under the auspices of the socialist publisher, Victor Gollancz. One of the most significant developments from this involvement with European aid was her relationship with a Hungarian psychologist and writer, Lilla Wagner. Roberts began a correspondence with Wagner, who had suffered imprisonment, persecution and hardship, in the immediate post-war period, and this developed into a mutually influential friendship that lasted more than twenty years. But her own lack of substantial income was becoming an increasing worry as she got older. She must have felt that the picture she had drawn in her very first published short story in 1918, 'Y Diafol yn 1960', of a penniless lonely old woman had been a premonition of her own fate. Fortunately, though, in 1958, Roberts became the recipient of a civil list pension, largely thanks to the lobbying of Saunders Lewis on her behalf. She wrote to thank him for his efforts on 24 March 1958, referring to his kindness as 'y gymwynas fwyaf a ddaeth imi yn yr adeg yma ar fy mywyd' (the greatest favour that has come my way at this stage of my life).[25] Roberts is a writer who never neglects the economic bases and imperatives of our lives; her own life was not lacking

1. Rhostryfan School in 1905. Kate Roberts is standing in the second row down, fourth from the left.

2. Students at the University College of North Wales, Bangor, 1913. Kate Roberts is second from the left in the back row.

3. Ystalyfera drama group, *c*.1917. Kate Roberts is bottom left, in the dark blouse.

4. Female teaching staff of Aberdare Girls' County School, early 1920s. Kate Roberts is in the back row, second from the left.

5. Studio portrait of Kate Roberts, Swansea, *c.*1918.

6. The newly married Kate Roberts and
   Morris T. Williams in the garden of 8 Lôn
   Isaf, Rhiwbina, *c.*1929

7. Morris T. Williams and Caradog Pritchard,
   Rhiwbina, *c.*1929.

in the struggle to 'get money to live', as she put it. It is fitting that her own achievements as a writer should have secured her the pension she needed to live out her long old age – and to continue writing.

Perhaps the advent of the civil list pension partly accounts for the geniality and *joie de vivre* of her next work. In *Te yn y Grug* (a volume of interlinked short stories), Roberts again returns to the world of childhood, as she had done in some of her earliest writing, such as *Deian a Loli*. The stories of *Te yn y Grug* have always been among Kate Roberts's most popular works, mainly because of their larger-than-life central character, Winni Ffinni Hadog. Roberts's skill at adopting the child's point of view and in bringing alive the immediacy of a child's perceptions is very much in evidence here, and was admired by reviewers and friends on publication. The anonymous reviewer in *Y Genhinen* (The Leek), for instance, described it as one of the most magical of her books and marvelled at her ability to 'mynd o dan groen plentyn fel hyn, a deall sut y mae ei feddwl yn gweithio' (get under the skin of a child in this way, and to understand how his mind works).[26] Roberts's friend and fellow short story writer, D. J. Williams, similarly, wrote to her in April 1959 to express his appreciation of the book. He particularly admires her ability to enter into the psychology of children, and her depiction of their crude honesty. He compares her work with his own, and finds the latter wanting – his own characters are too soft and, as Saunders Lewis once put it, so godly that they made him feel sick! There are certainly no nauseatingly godly characters in *Tea in the Heather*. This text has enjoyed popularity in its English translation as well and can be regarded as another of those works of the author's which are generically hybrid, being simultaneously both juvenile and adult fiction. There are elements of autobiography in *Te yn y Grug*, which perhaps account for the sense of authenticity that the text seems to exude. Its popularity may also be due to its humorous tone, a distinct change from Roberts's characteristic note of sadness.

The title story of the collection has Begw, the 8-year-old protagonist and, one suspects, a fictional projection of the author herself in her life 'before 1917', going for a picnic on the mountain-side with her friend, Mair. Roberts conveys Begw's intense sensual excitement and anticipation over the wonderful new invention that her mother has prepared for her to eat on the picnic: a bright, quivering red jelly in a long-stemmed glass. Mair's mother, the minister's wife, is dubious about letting the girls go alone to the mountain, since she is worried that they might be accosted by tramps. But the girls manage to escape and they are indeed ac-costed, by Winni Ffinni Hadog, a personage considerably more alarming for them than any tramp. Winni, a girl who swears like a trouper and is dressed in rags, most unlike the two 'proper' little girls, orders them to sit down on a patch of grass in the middle of the heather and proceeds to shock them with her talk. She reveals that she will go into service when she leaves school the following year and plans to go far away, perhaps to London. Her attitude towards her parents is disdainful and she has a defiant look on her face; for Begw, Winni becomes 'fel rhyw fath o broffwyd . . . yn edrych yr un fath â'r llun o Daniel yn ffau'r llewod' (a kind of prophet . . . looking just like the picture of Daniel in the lions' den).[27] Winni confesses to being a dreamer who often 'yn cael chwip din cyn mynd i 'ngwely' (has her arse whipped before going to bed).[28] Her audience of two are agog and horrified by the extremity of her language but Winni carries on obliviously, talking always of escape from her violent home. Her dream of freedom consists of becoming a maidservant to Queen Victoria herself:

A mi ga'i wisgo cap startsh gwyn ar ben fy shinón, a barclod gwyn, a llinynna hir 'dat odra fy sgert yn i glymu. A mi ga'i ffrog sidan i fynd allan gyda'r nos a breslet aur, a wats aur ar fy mrest yn sownd wrth froitsh aur cwlwm dolan a giard aur fawr yn ddau dro am fy ngwddw fi. A mi ga'i gariad del efo gwallt crychlyd, nid un 'r un fath â'r hen hogia coman sy fforma. A ffarwel i Twm Ffinni Hadog a'i wraig am byth bythoed.[29]

(I'll have a white starched cap on my chignon, and a white apron, and long strings down to the hem of my skirt to tie it. And I'll have a silk frock for going out at night and a gold bracelet, and a gold watch on

my breast fastened to a bow-knot brooch and a great gold chain in
two twists around my neck. And I'll have a handsome sweetheart
with curly hair, not one like these common old boys around here.
And farewell to Twm Finni Hadog and his wife forever.)

Winni's narrative is received very differently by the entranced
little girls and by the adult reader. We can see the poignancy of
Winni's dreams and the sadness of her circumstances, yet for
Mair and Begw she is a creature of almost boundless power, like
the prophet Daniel. Winni makes herself a crown from some
tendrils of fern and dances around, calling herself the 'Queen of
Sheba'. The painfully proper Begw cannot help but notice, as
Winni twirls around, that she is wearing no knickers under her
rags. Suddenly, though, Winni stops her dance, grabs Begw's
picnic and eats it all, including the longed-for jelly. 'A rŵan,' she
announces ''r ydw i am ych chwipio chi' (And now I'm going to
give you a thrashing).[30] After her beating, Begw escapes over the
mountain and lies down on a soft bed of moss, where she begins
to recuperate from her fright and disappointment:

> mor braf oedd bod ar wahân, yn lle bod ymysg pobl . . . Yr oedd y
> distawrwydd yma yn braf. Pob sŵn, sŵn o bell oedd o, sŵn cerrig yn
> mynd i lawr dros domen y chwarel, sŵn saethu Llanberis, bref dafad
> unig ymhell yn rhywle, a'r cwbl yn gwneud iddi feddwl am ochenaid
> y babi wrth gysgu yn ei grud gartref.[31]

> (how nice it was to be alone, instead of being among people . . . This
> silence was nice. Every sound was far away, the sound of stones
> tumbling down over a quarry tip, the sound of shot-firing from Llan-
> beris, the bleat of a lonely sheep far off somewhere, all of it making
> her think of the baby's sigh as he slept in his cradle at home.)

Despite the violence, a relationship is established between Begw
and Winni, whom she still admires; in later stories, though, when
Winni does go into service, she returns a very different, tamed
person: 'Nid yr un Winni ydy hi' (She isn't the same Winni),
thinks Begw.[32] The anarchic dreamer has been transformed into

someone who wears knickers and tidy clothes and goes to chapel on Sundays.

At about the same time as she was composing *Tegwch y Bore* and *Te yn y Grug* in the late 1950s, Kate Roberts had begun on another political campaign which would take up a significant portion of her later life. It is typical of the woman's irrepressible energy that, at the age of sixty-eight, when most people have retired and are settling into a quieter life, she dedicated herself to campaigning tirelessly for a Welsh-medium secondary school in Denbigh. This was a cause that was very close to Roberts's heart; having resented the Anglicized education which was imposed on her from an early age, and having spent much of her earlier adult life as a Welsh teacher, she now threw herself into this campaign. In 1973, Roberts stated, surprisingly, that the eventual success of this campaign, with the founding of Ysgol Twm o'r Nant, was the achievement in her life that made her feel most proud, outstripping even the sense of accomplishment given by her short stories: 'Cael Ysgol Gymraeg i Ddinbych ydy'r peth sydd wedi rhoi'r mwyaf o falchder i mi, nid fy straeon i' (Getting a Welsh school for Denbigh has made me feel the most proud, not my stories).[33] Today, with the burgeoning of Welsh-medium education, it is difficult to appreciate what a struggle the campaign for such a school was in the 1960s and 1970s. It was a hard battle but, in retrospect, it can be seen that the successful campaign led by Roberts laid many of the foundations for the much more prominent and popular role that the Welsh language has in primary and secondary education in Wales today.

While much of Roberts's fiction contains autobiographical elements, and she had spoken of her life in radio broadcasts and short essays, her next work, *Y Lôn Wen* (The White Lane; 1960) was her first and only full-length autobiography. It is subtitled *Darn o Hunangofiant* (A Fragment of Autobiography) and it takes the form of a series of 'pictures' of different aspects of Roberts's early life, along with descriptions of other family members and essays about the cultural history of Rhosgadfan. The text is therefore less a personal memoir than a portrayal of a family and a whole community, as indicated by the titles of some of the chapters: 'Diwylliant a'r Capel' (Culture and the Chapel) and 'Fy Mam' (My Mother). In fact, for an autobiographer, Roberts is noticeably reticent to say much about herself.

The first chapter, entitled 'Darluniau' (Pictures) is couched in the present tense and offers a series of vivid, chronological snapshots of the author's early childhood. When she visits her grandmother's house, the child's gaze takes in every detail of the interior and the garden:

> Mae dyrnau pres y dresel yn fy wynebu fel rhes o lygaid gloywon. Oddi ar y mur mae dau ewythr yn edrych arnaf o dan aeliau trymion . . . Mae cwrlid coch ar y bwrdd a Beibl mawr yn agored arno, sbectol ar y Beibl â'i breichiau wedi croesi fel coesau pry' . . . [Tu allan] mae cychod gwenyn ar un ochr fel nifer o dai bychain twt, ond nid wyf i fod i fynd yn agos atynt . . . Nid oes ardd debyg i hon yn unlle. Mae fel llyfr wedi ei gau efo chlesbin.[34]

> (The brass knobs of the dresser face me like a row of glistening eyes. From the wall two uncles look down at me from beneath their heavy brows . . . There's a red cloth on the table and a big Bible is open on it, a pair of spectacles on the Bible with its arms crossed like the legs of an insect . . . [Outside] there are beehives along one side like a line of neat little houses, but I'm not supposed to go near them . . . There's no garden like this one anywhere else. It's like a book with a clasp to close it.)

Despite her enjoyment of her grandmother's house, the old woman is strict and makes the young Kate feel inadequate; she reminds her that at her age (ten) her mother had been sent away as a maidservant. Other memories in these fragmented pictures are of the dead body of a quarryman being carried past on a cart; a cold evening in the Seiat with people 'speaking their experience' ('yn dweud eu profiadau'); the community coming together for haymaking and choir practices; the death of a calf, at which her mother cries. Above all, she remembers the white lane of the title, which leads towards the highest mountains:

Yr ydym yn dringo ac yn dringo nes cyrraedd Pen 'Rallt Fawr. Yr ydym yn gweld reit at Bont y Borth, ond yn gweld peth arall na fedrwn byth ei weld o'n tŷ ni – y Lôn Wen, sy'n mynd dros Foel Smatho i'r Waun-fawr ac i'r Nefoedd.[35]

(We climb and climb until we reach Pen 'Rallt Fawr. We can see as far as Borth Bridge, but we can also see something else that we can't see at all from our house – the White Lane, which goes over Moel Smatho to Waun-fawr and to Heaven.)

Roberts adopts a very different, adult, academic tone in the narrative of 'Fy Ardal' (My Neighbourhood), drawing on historical research about the founding of the villages of Rhosgadfan and Rhostryfan. The text becomes almost a social history of the area, animated by detailed personal recollections. The interpenetration of literary and real landscapes is suggested by Roberts's remark that when she first read *Wuthering Heights* she immediately thought of her own native region.[36]

In *Y Lôn Wen*, we can see Kate Roberts, by now a widow in her late sixties, attempting to chronicle not just a disappearing world but one which had, she felt, in many senses already disappeared. The last chapter of *Y Lôn Wen*, entitled 'Y Darlun Olaf' (The Last Picture) is particularly poignant in its shift from the lovingly remembered past to the diminished present. She reflects:

Pan fûm yn ysgrifennu'r pethau hyn fe gododd y meirw o'u beddau am ysbaid i siarad efo mi. Fe ânt yn ôl i gysgu eto. Ysgrifennais am fy nheulu a'i alw'n hunangofiant, ond yr wyf yn iawn. Fy hanes i fy hun yw hanes fy nheulu . . . Digwyddasai popeth pwysig i mi cyn 1917, popeth dwfn ei argraff.[37]

(As I wrote these things the dead arose from their graves for a while to talk to me. They will go back to sleep now. I have written about my family and called it an autobiography but that description is accurate. My own history is the history of my family . . . Everything important happened to me before 1917, everything which made a lasting impression.)

In this moving final chapter, Roberts converses with the dead who rise from their graves but, in a deeper sense, the memoir is about childhood. The child that Kate Roberts was before 1917 is the child who comes to life in the early 'pictures' of *Y Lôn Wen*. And that child is still vividly alive in Kate Roberts the elderly woman, still asking questions on the last page of the book.

5

'This stiff, indomitable queen of Welsh letters': 1960–1985

In this final period of her life, we see Kate Roberts responding to the transformed circumstances of modern Wales, attempting to come to grips with a society increasingly Anglicized and secularized. Her prose never lapses into sentimentality; on the contrary, the later stories retain an unflinching verisimilitude. She writes both about the experience of being an old woman in a society which is brutally uncaring of its elderly and, at the same time, turns to examine the lives of children with penetrating insight. In texts such as the novella, *Tywyll Heno* and the final volumes of short stories, *Yr Wylan Deg* (The Fair Seagull) and *Haul a Drycin* (Sunshine and Storm), she shows that, though she regrets the passing of that lost Welsh world pre-1917, she always as an artist responded to and wrote of the changing circumstances of the present.

Tywyll Heno (1962) is a novella which brings the reader uncomfortably close to what it must feel like to experience a mental breakdown. The novelist, Islwyn Ffowc Elis, reviewed it in the journal *Lleufer* (Illumination) claiming that 'Nid ei harddull yw ei chryfder. Ei chryfder yw ei hamgyffred eithriadol o sefyllfa a chymeriad . . . Er gwaetha'i harddull y mae hi'n llenor mawr, nid o'i herwydd' (Her strength is not her style. Her strength is her exceptional grasp of situation and character . . . It is in spite of her style that she is a great author, not because of it).[1] This is a surprising and surely inaccurate judgement, contrasting starkly with the view of Saunders Lewis, for instance, who frequently expressed his admiration of Roberts's style. Nevertheless, Elis is right in praising her 'exceptional grasp of situation and character' in this particular text.

The novella is a first-person narrative in the voice of Bet Jones, a minister's wife, whom we first meet as a patient in the ward of a large psychiatric hospital. The narrative is a retrospective one, recounting the trajectory which brought Bet to a mental break-down. She describes the process as a 'loss of faith' but this should not be interpreted in a purely religious sense. Roberts almost never writes about religious experience and her interest in the chapel here, as elsewhere in her oeuvre, is as a social institution. Bet's 'loss of faith' is really a descent into depression, in which she is unable to see any meaning or purpose in life. Reminiscent of Sylvia Plath's description of mental illness in her contempor-aneous novel, *The Bell Jar*, *Tywyll Heno* renders Bet's illness as something that takes over her body from within: 'fe aeth y di-galondid . . . yn fwgwd am fy mhen; yn glwt o dduwch; yn rhew; yn niwl; yn bwysau wrth fy nghalon a'r pwysau ar fin torri a disgyn' (the unhappiness became . . . a mask over my face; a black cloth; ice; fog; a weight on my heart about to break and fall to pieces).[2] Although the pettiness of chapel society, especially the meanly vindictive womenfolk, is something that Bet finds hard to bear, fundamentally it is not outward circumstance that causes her breakdown but an existential crisis that comes from within.

Bet's cosmopolitan friend, Melinda, is able to escape from the narrowness of her life to the freedom and sensual pleasure of Paris. The relationship between the two women is very close, verging on the erotic; Bet admires her friend's beauty and longs for her ability to ignore the narrowness of small town life. Bet's only escape, tell-ingly, is through writing. In this regard, at least, Bet is an author-ial alter ego, using her writing as self-therapy to emerge from the suffocating mask of despair. Unusually, Roberts uses a number of literary allusions and parallels in this work, notably the anonym-ous ninth-century Welsh poems known as 'Canu Heledd' (The Songs of Heledd), which are moving elegies composed in a first-person female voice. Bet contrasts these poems and the voice of Heledd, with whom she empathizes completely, to the voice of the mystic writer, Morgan Llwyd, in his allegorical work *Llyfr y Tri*

Aderyn (The Book of the Three Birds; 1653), which offers a promise of God's guidance and enlightenment to the wavering soul. As Bet reflects, 'Hawdd oedd dweud bod y Goruchaf yn galw'r goleuni allan o'r tywyllwch. Ond sut? . . . teimlwn fy mod yn perthyn yn nes i Heledd nag i Morgan Llwyd' (It was easy to say that the Almighty called light forth from the darkness. But how? . . . I felt that I was more closely related to Heledd than to Morgan Llwyd).[3] Once again, despite existing in a male-dominated world of Welsh letters, Roberts shows her desire to belong to a female tradition of literary expression. Like her author, Bet survives, finally breaking through the debilitating and silencing mask of her depression.

Roberts's next publication, *Hyn o Fyd* (A World Such as This; 1964), contains just five stories, ranging from 'Yr Atgyfodiad' (The Resurrection) at only four pages to 'Teulu Mari' (Mari's family) which, at thirty-six pages, is almost a novella. In his review of this volume, Saunders Lewis juxtaposes Kate Roberts's succinctness and austerity with Simone de Beauvoir's prolixity and excess (he refers specifically to her massive, three-volume autobiography) while also acknowledging similarities between the two female writers. He sees Roberts here in Yeatsian mode, 'cast[ing] a cold eye/on life, on death' and he ends by offering an image of an isolated old woman who 'lives for her writing, this stiff, indomitable queen of Welsh letters'.[4] Lewis is clearly making Kate Roberts into a kind of 'monument of unageing intellect', such as the older Yeats longed to be.[5] This apotheosis was, however, premature. The stiff queen had plenty of life in her yet, and she would go on, not only to publish a further four volumes of short fiction in her lifetime, but to fight a successful public battle to gain Welsh-medium education for children in Denbigh. To some extent Roberts became, like Yeats the senator in the new Irish free state, a 'sixty-year-old smiling public [wo]man', except that in Roberts's case there was less smiling and more gritting of teeth.[6]

Jerry Hunter offers an extremely detailed analysis of 'Yr Atgyfodiad', the shortest story from this 1964 collection in the annual lecture given to the Friends of Cae'r Gors (the community centre established as a memorial to Kate Roberts in her childhood home), published in 2005. The analysis is about five times as long as 'The Resurrection' itself. Hunter sees the story as an attempt to write about the unspeakable: to write after the Holocaust and the terrible sufferings of the Second World War. He, like other recent commentators, such as Nia Williams and Francesca Rhydderch, points to the key importance of Roberts's friendship with the Hungarian writer and psychoanalyst, Lilla Wagner, from immediately after the war until the late 1960s.[7] Wagner herself had been persecuted and had suffered from hardship and want in the war and during the later 1940s; Roberts had helped her materially by sending food and clothing, but the lengthy correspondence between the two women shows that Wagner also helped Roberts, giving her an insight into what was happening in Europe and, crucially, enhancing her understanding of human psychology. 'Yr Atgyfodiad' focuses on the lone female figure who becomes increasingly central in Roberts's later works (in contrast to the families and married couples of the earlier period) and adopts a journal form which affords scope for a very intimate, stream-of-consciousness style. Hunter suggests that in the experimentalism of her style in this story, Roberts begins to try to accomplish what Adorno said is the role of avant-garde art after the Holocaust: to bear witness, to tell the truth, to begin to speak of the unspeakable. Arguably, though, this is merely a continuation of what Roberts has been doing throughout her career as a writer.

Hyn o Fyd also contains a well-known story by Kate Roberts which has featured, in translation, in a number of anthologies, namely 'Cathod mewn Ocsiwn' (Cats at an Auction). She was always interested in the auction as a plot device (it is used, for example, in the 1937 story, 'The Quilt'), perhaps because it offers a resonant metaphor for the transience of life while at the same time foregrounding the material objects which condition existence. The story opens with Elen wondering whether to attend the sale of furniture at the deceased Mrs Hughes's house or not. She has always wanted a corner cupboard and has heard that Mrs Hughes possessed one but, after all these years, her desire has diminished and she is in two minds. The reader is taken very close to the consciousness of Elen as she ponders, elaborating an extended simile between the corner cupboard and a late, unexpected and un-wanted child. But, by the end of the opening paragraph, Elen has determined to go, since 'weithiau fe ddoid i garu'r plentyn an-nisgwyl yn fwy na'r lleill' (sometimes one grows to love the un-expected child more than the others).[8] This displacement of desire and quasi-maternal affection onto household objects is a par-ticularly stark example of a common trope in Roberts's work: a woman's domestic sphere becomes something loved for itself, an emblem of identity and continuity, in lieu of the possibility of fulfillment elsewhere.

But Elen is reluctant to go: she cannot help thinking about the deceased Mrs Hughes, a drab, unremarkable woman in her sixties about whom people are now beginning to relish gossiping. The dead woman's house turns out to be dirty and ill-kempt, and the female 'cats' at the auction enjoy expressing their astonishment at the state of the place. Elen feels a moment of pity and fellow-feeling for the dead woman, but hardens her heart and sets out to secure the cupboard. In the bidding, though, she lets herself be defeated by an eager young married woman, though she wants to buy the cupboard now not for herself but in memory of the poor, bland Mrs Hughes, whose catty friends now betray her. Staring pensively at a rolled-up carpet, Elen sees in it an image of the dead Mrs Hughes lying pale in her coffin; the state of her house indicates to the obsessively house-proud Elen that something had snapped in her – she had given up on life: 'Roedd y ddynas wedi'i gorchfygu' (the woman had been defeated).[9] Once again, as in other stories, such as 'Sisters', the struggle to keep domestic order is seen as a triumph over the adverse circumstances of women's lives. Elen is determined to maintain this order against the chaos and degeneration all around her: she will keep her children/ furniture together, no matter what.

Roberts's next publication after *Hyn o Fyd* was *Tegwch y Bore* in 1967; though this novel had appeared in serialized form a decade previously, it had not appeared as a single volume before. Soon after, Roberts wrote to Saunders Lewis to thank him for his praise of the novel and simply for continuing to remember her: 'Mae pobl yn anghofio hen bobl, ac yn mynegi syndod ein bod yn byw o hyd. "Diar, ydi hi'n fyw o hyd, 'roeddwn i'n meddwl bod hi wedi marw ers talwm?" Dyna'r agwedd. Yr ydych chi yn fyw iawn beth bynnag' (People forget about old people, and express their astonishment that they are still alive. 'Dear me, is she still alive, I thought she'd died long ago?' That's the attitude. At any rate, you are very much alive).[10] Actually, both she and Saunders would live for another seventeen years. Both died, within six months of each other, in 1985.

To mark the fact that she was still, like Saunders, 'very much alive', she brought out another volume of stories in 1969. *Prynu Dol a Storïau Eraill* (Buying a Doll and other Stories), her fourteenth published volume, contains nine stories. The title of one, 'Yr Enaid Clwyfus' (The Wounded Soul) has been taken from this collection to give its name to a volume in tribute to Roberts's work by John Emyr in 1976. The critic evidently saw the title as being applicable to Roberts herself, and it is easy to see why. The story concerns an old man in a mental hospital, simply waiting for something to happen. Roberts has a recurring interest in mental illness and disability, which is there from the very earliest stories, such as 'Henaint'. In this regard, she can be seen to belong to a canon of women's writing which explores the issue of madness as one with particular relevance to women's lives. *Tywyll Heno* is perhaps her most thorough and brilliant exploration of mental illness; this brief story, though, shows that Roberts is acutely aware that men can also be the victims of such illness (the earlier story, 'Yr Athronydd', is another example).

'Y Crys Glan' (The Clean Shirt) has an urban setting and is concerned with the lives of young printers. The main protagonist, Glyn, has managed to get a clean shirt by washing it himself, though he is forced to live in squalor, his parents being drunkards with many children. He loves Mari, and the story shows them triumphing over adverse circumstances. It is interesting how often Roberts uses laundry as a symbol of victory over poverty and hardship. It is as if the sheer hard labour of washing and the transformation of something soiled into something clean and bright stands for the possibilities of the triumph of the human soul.

'Prynu Dol' (Buying a Doll), the title story, features an old woman who buys a doll in order to dress her in some beautiful, hand-made clothes that she herself had sewn some fifty years previously. The doll becomes an image of the old woman herself as a child. Standing in refutation of Islwyn Ffowc Elis's derogation of Roberts's style, this story contains the most exquisite description of the intricacy of the needlework in the doll's clothes:

> Pais wlanen wen a band cialico wedi ei phwytho efo edau las. Dau fath o wnïad, un yn troi ar ei gilydd, a'r llall yn troi oddi wrth ei gilydd, wedi eu gwneud efo pwyth rhedeg a phwyth croes. Pleten ar ei godre, a'r top wedi ei bletio i'r band. Rhes o bwythi ôl ar y band, yn fanach nag y gallai unrhyw beiriant gwnïo eu gwneud . . . Brat hollol blaen o gotyn na welwyd mo'i debyg byth wedyn. Cefndir gwyn â sprigyn bach o flodyn coch arno. Nid oedd crychu yn hwn. Rhedai rhuban gwyn cul drwy hem y gwddw, hem ffug a dorasid ar groes, ac mor gul, fel ei bod yn anodd gwybod sut yr aeth y rhuban drwyddi a llwyddo i grychu a chau yn dynn am y gwddw.[11]

> (A white flannel petticoat with a calico waistband stitched with a blue thread. Two kinds of sewing, one row turning inwards and the other outwards, done with a running stitch and a cross stitch. A pleat along the hem, and the top folded into the waistband. A row of backstitch on the waistband, smaller than any sewing machine could ever manage . . . A plain cotton apron of a quality never seen since. A white background with a sprig of tiny red flowers on it. This garment had no smocking. A narrow white ribbon ran through the neckline, which had a false hem cut on the bias, and so narrow that it was hard to credit how the ribbon could go through it and succeed in being gathered and tied tightly at the neck.)

This story again can be seen as a celebration of women's work, women's craftsmanship, as well as of the beauty of a language whose words are beginning to be forgotten. Clothing, once more, becomes the source of the most powerful symbolism in Roberts's work.

In 'Blodau' (Flowers) Gwen Huws, who is 94 years old and on her death bed, is visited by Mrs Jones, wife of the coffin-maker. Gwen gives her short shrift, informing her that Mr Ryan will be making her coffin. Mrs Jones has brought carnations in March, which both Gwen and her neighbour, Leusa, believe have been stolen from the crematorium. Gwen is happy to be at home, and not in the hospital. She likes listening to Leusa getting on with the domestic tasks – this is reminiscent of the dying character, Dafydd, in 'Y Condemniedig', who takes comfort from listening to his wife working. Gwen thinks about chapel-goers such as herself and their flaws; in her mind she says goodbye: 'Diflannodd y cymeriadau o un i un yn llwyd dros y gorwel, y hi yn olaf, yn codi ei llaw arni hi ei hun wrth ddiflannu' (The characters disappeared one by one over the horizon, she herself the last, raising her hand in farewell to herself as she disappeared).[12] In conversation with Mr Davies the minister, they discuss what would be nice to have as a last view before death; Davies mentions that a teacher he had known longed to have a last glimpse of the river Menai. Gwen, though, unromantic to the last, would like as her last glimpse of life: 'ryw gadach llestri braf, fuo'n help i mi ruthro 'mlaen efo ngwaith' (some fine dishcloth that was a help to me in rushing ahead with my work).[13] Again, the focus is on domestic labour, which seems to have a defining function for female identity in Roberts's writing.

'Y Daith' (The Journey) hearkens back to the past, since it is set in 1912, when Dafydd, the youngest son of the family, leaves home for the 'Sowth'. Both this and 'Dewis Bywyd' (Choosing a Life) have evident autobiographical elements – the latter even mentions the deaths of the protagonist's brother and husband. Both focus on 'ing hiraeth' (the anguish of longing/homesickness). 'Brwydr efo'r Nadolig' (A Struggle with Christmas) is in diary form. Somewhat reminiscent of 'Meddyliau Siopwr' (A Shopkeeper's Thoughts) from the earlier collection, *Rhigolau Bywyd* (1929), and 'Cwsmeriaid' (Customers) in *Yr Wylan Deg* (1976), in this story, too, the narrator is a shopkeeper. Roberts reveals how the male shopkeeper can have a privileged, and often unwanted, insight into the private lives of his female customers. Finally, 'Dau Hen Ddyn' (Two Old Men) starts with a coffin being carried into the chapel, with eighty-eight years engraved on its plate. Nathan Huws, seventy-eight years old, watches. The dead man, Wil Dic, was a miser, and now that he is dead his relatives descend on the funeral 'like a flock of starlings on a harvested field'. Nathan, like a number of the characters in this late volume, is a writer, perhaps an authorial alter ego – all such characters are acutely perceptive but remain detached and lonely.

Gobaith a Storïau Eraill (Hope and Other Stories) published by Gwasg Gee in 1972 is not exclusively a volume of stories from this period. Rather, it is a collection of stories from earlier stages of Roberts's career, gleaned from various periodicals and news-papers, such as *Y Faner*, *Barn* and *Taliesin*. 'Gwacter' (Emptiness) is not the same story as the one which appears under that title in the later volume, *Haul a Drycin* (1981), though both centre on a female character and are in diary form. Clearly, the notion of emptiness and the parallel one of surfeit are states of anomie which tend to afflict Roberts's female protagonists from the late 1940s onwards. Neverthless, the title of the collection is 'Hope', rather than 'Emptiness', so we should perhaps view this collection, like so many of Roberts's writings in old age as a celebration of survival and persistence, despite the odds.

The title story has Sal Huws as its centre of consciousness: she and her husband, Huw, have been married for twelve years before she becomes pregnant. A fine baby boy is born but a few months later the doctor explains that the child is 'not right in the head'. Caring for this disabled child has opposing effects on his mother and father: Sal comes to idolize him, while Huw is repulsed by him, and increasingly jealous. The story is in free indirect style, intensely focalized on Sal's conflicting thoughts, as she sits outside with the child, Iolo, who is now four years old and has yet to say a word. She regrets the memorably described 'fan ffraeo draenogaidd, di-dor derfyn' (endless, hedgehogish bickering) that her relationship with her husband has decended into, but she still retains hope that her son will one day speak.[14] They sit outside in the 'iron' intensity of July sunshine, watching the antics of a pig in a nearby field.

Suddenly, Iolo points to the animal and utters the word 'Nioch' (onomatopoeia for a pig's grunt), thereafter repeating it again and again.[15] Sal's hope against the odds appears to have been vindicated and the story ends with her crying with happiness. The story's ending, though, is typically open, since Huw's reaction remains unnarrated and unpredictable.

'Y Trysor' (The Treasure) also focuses on one woman's thoughts: Jane Rhisiart is now seventy-two and reflects that she has sat down like this to review her life four times to date. The first time was when, at the age of twenty-five, her husband left her and disappeared. The second was twenty years later, her three children grown up and married; the third time was five years after that when she gave up her smallholding and went to live next to her friend, Martha. And the fourth, the 'now' of the story, is twelve years later, soon after the death of Martha. This is a story which privileges the close friendships of older women over marital relationships: Jane reflects that when her good-for-nothing husband abandoned the family, she had the sympathy of the entire neighbourhood, while she was secretly quite glad to see him go. Now, however, when the 'treasure' of her later life has died, the only person in her life whom she has ever been able to talk to intimately and with mutual regard, other people think nothing of it. Jane is suffering the most intense grief of her life and is unable to express it. This is a story characteristic of the later works of Roberts in its focus on the isolation of old age and the impossibility of human communication. As always, though, there is a fine balance between that desolate picture of the solitary old lady and the knowledge that she still retains about the warmth of the love she has experienced, though it is now lost.

The lives of old people also take centre stage in the 1976 collection, *Yr Wylan Deg a Storïau Eraill*. 'Hen Bobl yn Caru' (Old People Courting) is a framed story in which Siân narrates a love story to an audience of elderly women in an old people's home. The description of the old ladies is a masterpiece of telling observation, such as their wearing of obligatory cardigans in pastel colours, their carrying of handbags which are over-stuffed as if they dare not leave anything in their rooms, and their wearing of necklaces which fail to conceal the hanging flesh of old age on their necks. Moreover, they are reduced to their first names only, as if all other markers of identity have been denied them: Lisi, Mari, Winni and so on line up eagerly to hear the story. Only one of their number is missing: Doli, who is alleged to be courting Bob Huws, much to the other ladies' amusement. The story within the story is a happy romance (uncharacteristic of Roberts's stories) dealing with a couple coming together in old age; half the audience is satisfied by the story, while the other half do not like the focus on old people in love. In fact, Magi expresses physical disgust at the thought of old people 'making love when their flesh is starting to rot' ('yn caru a'u cnawd wedi dechrau pydru'[16]). The intensity of this self-disgust is striking but is contested by other members of the audience who value the story's focus on friendship and companionship. One of the many effects of this strikingly original story is to re-endow the old women in the home with individuality and difference; bereft of their own homes, stripped of their old surnames, they are yet lively and distinctive human beings with dissenting opinions about life. At the same time, the story functions, cleverly, as a self-reflexive critique on the art of the short story. Kate Roberts may have been herself a very old lady when she wrote this story, well into her eighties, yet she shows her continuing command of the short story genre and her willingness to address taboo subjects, such as sexual relationships in old age. In fact, Roberts's work becomes more daring in this regard, surprisingly, as she enters her ninth decade. This is shown, for instance in another story in this collection, 'Yn Ôl Eto' (Back Again), narrated by Mr Edwards, a chapel minister, who is privy to the most secret confessions and desires of members of his congregation. One old lady of eighty-five confides in him when he visits her in hospital that she would feel considerably better if she could have a man in bed with her. Similarly, Sam, a young teacher who has taken a year off from his dismal job to be a simple tramp, reveals that on his travels he has been propositioned many times, for instance by a young woman who tells him that her husband is away for the night and suggestively gives him some money. In this way, the strength of female sexual desire in old and young alike is foregrounded in a much more open way than in any of Roberts's earlier works. It is tempting to see this greater candour as a symptom of the way in which old age can, paradoxically, liberate one from the duties and proprieties of one's life, an extreme example being the old woman in the very early story 'Henaint' who has forgotten everything and therefore has no cares or inhibitions.

The interpolated story in 'Hen Bobl yn Caru' bears strong similarities to the plot of *Modryb a Nith*, discussed earlier. This self-reflexivity suggests that Roberts was still open to experiment even at this late stage in her writing career. Although she felt herself to have been 'forgotten', the correspondence in the National Library of Wales shows that she continued to receive many letters of admiration and appreciation at this stage in her life. Aneirin Talfan Davies, for instance, writes in admiration of her work, comparing the stories of *Yr Wylan Deg* favourably with those of Joyce's *Dubliners*, concluding that all of Wales owes her a debt of gratitude for continuing to write.[17]

Haul a Drycin, published in 1981, was the last collection of stories to appear in Roberts's lifetime. It consists of only six short stories, for which the author herself apologizes poignantly in the foreword, where she states that she failed to write any more on account of illness.[18] The fact that she was 90 years old at the time and still felt the need to apologize speaks volumes for the author's formidable sense of duty and tenacity. The six stories in the volume are: 'Pryder Morwyn' (A Maid's Worry), 'Haul a Drycin' (Sunshine and Storm), 'Dechrau Byw' (Starting to Live), 'Gwacter' (Emptiness), 'Maggie' and 'O! Winni! Winni!' Three of the six stories concern the adolescent Winni Ffinni Hadog (the character introduced in the earlier volume, *Te yn y Grug*) and her life as a servant girl in the town. Her life continues to be shadowed by her tyrannical drunken father, Twm, who steals her money and exploits her. She takes refuge with Elin Gruffydd, a substitute mother. Elin's daughter, Begw, who was central to the stories of

Te yn y Grug is present here but has a very marginal role – Winni herself is the centre of consciousness. The three other stories concern visits to hospital, reflections perhaps of Roberts's own increasing frailty and experience of ill-health, anxiety and dependence on others. These are sad stories but they also have pulses of energy and hope in them, for example 'Gwacter', written in the form of a diary, has the ailing first-person speaker seek meaning in the emptiness of her life through writing a love story, with which she becomes obsessed and, while she is composing the story, she identifies completely with its young protagonist: 'daeth Jane a minnau'n un, cymerais i ei lle' (Jane and I became one, I took her place).[19] Through imagination she is young and hopeful again. Winni performs a similar function, though Winni is an anti-heroine, who may be construed as a dark double to Kate Roberts. Like Bertha Rochester, she often acts out the transgressive behaviour not allowed to Roberts's 'good' Jane Eyre characters, like Begw. Winni is full of desire – impulsive, outspoken, angry, unconventional, pugnacious, ungodly, but she is held down by a brutal patriarchy which even well-meaning characters cannot gainsay. Twm, her father, continues to steal her money and treat her as a chattel. Sadly, even the little half-brother upon whom she dotes is growing to be like his bullying father by the end of the final story, suggesting that patriarchy is by no means a thing of the past.

As previously mentioned, dogs appear frequently in these later stories, described tenderly and often appearing as child substitutes. There is a moment in 'Pryder Morwyn', for example, where Winni encounters a kindly neighbour and his dog on the mountain, and the sole purpose of this encounter seems to be to show how similar the dog's expression is to a child's. While Winni's parents are vicious and neglectful, the dog/infant is full of tenderness and understanding: 'Gwrandawai'r ci fel petai'n deall y cwbl, a sylwodd Winni ar ei llygaid ffeind, mor wahanol i lygaid ei thad a'i llys-fam y prynhawn yma ac mor debyg i lygaid Sionyn' (The dog listened as if he understood it all, and Winni noticed his gentle eyes, so different from those of her father and stepmother that afternoon and so like little Sionyn's eyes).[20]

'Dechrau Byw' focuses on 20-year-old Deina Prys, who is just married. She sits by the fire and remembers – her story, a love story, is told through her unspoken reminiscences. She takes delight in her comfortable hearth, remembering herself as a young wife taking pride in her new home after the difficulties of choosing as her husband the man whom her sisters thought not good enough for her. Possibly there are echoes here of the relationship between Roberts herself and her husband, for Deina seems to be somewhat older than Harri. She has also acted as his teacher, helping him to become literate. She comes from a higher social class, while he is a workhouse boy, a former servant in her family and her sisters therefore disapprove. But the story is also historical, reflecting the period when the quarries were just beginning to be exploited in Caernarfonshire, chapels were just being built and tea was a rare delicacy. The story bears strong similarities to the historical drama entitled *Y Gwas*, among Roberts's papers and discussed above. These different generic versions of the same material demonstrate that Roberts was an inveterate experimenter. In this case, the story is more successful than the play, perhaps because Roberts was by now very much a mistress of the short story genre. Over the past half a century, she had made it her own, establishing an important tradition of short fiction in Wales which continues to this day. She had also produced a handful of novels which are among the classics of the genre in twentieth-century Wales, along with a very large body of non-fiction writing that has yet to be fully explored and appreciated.

* * *

On 14 April 1985, Kate Roberts died. She was ninety-four years old. Her biography was the stuff of her writing but, in keeping with her favoured sartorial imagery, she stitched and altered and embellished that raw material into an infinite number of different forms. Her contemporary Jean Rhys (whose father, William Rees Williams was also, coincidentally, from Caernarfonshire) could admit 'not that my books are entirely my life – but almost'; the deeply reticent Kate Roberts would never have made such an admission, yet her life is just as much at the root of her work.[21] We do not meet in her stories the 'Kate Roberts heroine', as we do the recurring, poignant 'Jean Rhys heroine' in the latter writer's fiction; Roberts has greater range and empathy than her Caribbean contemporary, distilling her own experiences, desires, fears and memories into a range of disparate and memorable characters – grandfathers, widows, bachelors, children, old women, servant girls, wives, husbands, shopkeepers, quarrymen, mothers, even animals – like the cheeky calf in 'The Widow' or the sympathetic dog in 'The Worries of a Servant-girl'.

On the face of it, Kate Roberts led quite a circumscribed life. She travelled little, lived all her life in Wales, had no children and struggled to make ends meet. Viewed from a Welsh perspective, though, her profile grows: she achieved early critical acclaim for her literary works; she was an influential teacher, numbering perhaps the greatest Welsh poet of the century, Gwenallt, among her pupils; she was a committed and effective political campaigner on behalf of Plaid Cymru and on behalf of Welsh-medium education; she was a prolific journalist and publisher; a prominent figure in the chapel and the Eisteddfod; a recipient of honorary degrees, a civil list pension, extravagantly positive reviews. Finally, she achieved apotheosis as 'the queen of our literature'. Yet, since her death a quarter of a century ago, her reputation seems to have ossified. She is acknowledged as an important figure but only a handful of her works continue to be read. Despite her devotion to Wales and to the Welsh language, she certainly saw herself as participating in a 'world republic of letters', which included Woolf and Chekhov as well as Saunders Lewis and Daniel Owen. Now that more of her work is becoming available in translation, the time is right for the rediscovery of Roberts's writing, not only in Wales but across the British Isles and the rest of Europe and America.

Notes

1

1   'Digwyddasai popeth pwysig i mi cyn 1917, popeth dwfn ei argraff.' See Kate Roberts, *Y Lôn Wen* (Denbigh: Gee, 1960), p. 30.
2   Owen M. Edwards, *Wales* (The Story of the Nations Series) (London: T. Fisher Unwin; New York: G. P. Puttnam's Sons, 1907), p. 8.
3   Estyn Evans, *The Personality of Wales*, BBC Wales Annual Radio Lecture (Cardiff: BBC Wales, 1973), p. 10.
4   Kate Roberts, *Atgofion*, vol. 1 (Porthmadog: Gwasg Tŷ ar y Graig, 1972), p. 15.
5   Ibid., p. 26.
6   Alan Llwyd and Elwyn Edwards, *Y Bardd a Gollwyd* (Swansea: Barddas, 1992), pp. 19–20.
7   Ifor Williams, Letter of recommendation dated 7 April 1927; attached to a typed CV of Kate Roberts dated 1934, NLW Kate Roberts Papers 2807.
8   Roberts, *Atgofion*, p. 29.
9   Nia Williams, '"Fy iaith, fy ngwlad, fy nghenedl": hanes ymgyrch-oedd gwleidyddol Kate Roberts 1915–1961' (MA thesis, University of Wales, Aberystwyth, 1998), 33.
10 See Francesca Rhydderch, 'Cultural translations: a comparative critical study of Kate Roberts and Virginia Woolf' (Ph.D. thesis, University of Wales, Aberystwyth, 2001).

2

1   Kate Roberts, 'Y Diafol yn 1960', *Y Darian*, 21 November 1918, p. 3.
2   Kate Roberts, Letter to Saunders Lewis, 23 January 1923, NLW Kate Roberts and Saunders Lewis correspondence 22723D, ff. 1–2; reproduced in *Annwyl Kate, Annwyl Saunders: Gohebiaeth 1923–1983*, ed. Dafydd Ifans (Aberystwyth: Llyfrgell Genedlaethol Cymru, 1992), p. 2.

[3]   L. P. Nemo, Letter to Kate Roberts from Brest, Brittany, dated 30 December 1925, NLW Kate Roberts Papers 78.

[4]   Kate Roberts, 'Yr Athronydd', *O Gors y Bryniau* (1925; Caerdydd: Hughes a'i fab, 1992), p. 36.

[5]   Kate Roberts, 'Newid Byd', *O Gors y Bryniau* (1925; Caerdydd: Hughes a'i fab, 1992), p. 46.

[6]   Ibid., pp. 48–9.

[7]   Kate Roberts, 'Pryfocio', *O Gors y Bryniau* (1925; Caerdydd: Hughes a'i fab, 1992), p. 63.

[8]   Ibid., p. 65.

[9]   Kate Roberts, 'Y wraig weddw', *O Gors y Bryniau* (1925; Caerdydd: Hughes a'i fab, 1992), p. 73.

[10] Ibid., p. 78.

[11] Kate Roberts, Letter to Saunders Lewis, 11 October 1923, NLW Kate Roberts and Saunders Lewis correspondence 22723D ff. 5–12; reproduced in *Annwyl Kate, Annwyl Saunders*, p. 5.

[12] Kate Roberts, Letter to Saunders Lewis, 11 February 1927, NLW Kate Roberts and Saunders Lewis correspondence 22723D ff. 18–20; reproduced in ibid., p. 17.

[13] Kate Roberts, Letter to Saunders Lewis, 11 October 1923, NLW Kate Roberts and Saunders Lewis correspondence 22723D ff. 5–12; reproduced in ibid., p. 6.

[14] Kate Roberts, Letter to Saunders Lewis, 4 April 1927, NLW Kate Roberts and Saunders Lewis correspondence 22723D ff. 21–2; reproduced in ibid., p. 20.

[15] Kate Roberts, 'Cosbi', *Deian a Loli* (1927; Cardiff: Hughes & Son, 1992), p. 53.

[16] Ibid.

[17] Mihangel Morgan, 'Kate yn y cwm', in Hywel Teifi Edwards (ed.), *Cwm Cynon* (Llandysul: Gomer, 1997), pp. 285–308.

[18] John Emyr, Introduction to Kate Roberts, *Deian a Loli* (1927; Cardiff: Hughes & Son, 1992), p. x.

[19] Kate Roberts, *Deian a Loli* (1927; Cardiff: Hughes & Son, 1992), p. 25.

[20] Ibid., p. 70.

[21] Saunders Lewis, Letter to Kate Roberts, October 1923, NLW Kate Roberts Papers 64; reproduced in *Annwyl Kate, Annwyl Saunders*, pp. 4–5.

[22] Eigra Lewis Roberts, *Kate Roberts: Llên y Llenor* (Caernarfon: Gwasg Pantycelyn, 1994), p. 16.

[23] Kate Roberts, Letter to Saunders Lewis, 3 April 1931, NLW Kate Roberts and Saunders Lewis correspondence 22723D ff. 85–8; reproduced in *Annwyl Kate, Annwyl Saunders*, pp. 77–8.

24 Siân Williams, Letter to Kate Roberts, undated [probably January 1929], NLW Kate Roberts Papers 119.
25 Twenty-one letters from Kate Roberts to Morris T. Williams between 1926 and 1931, NLW Kate Roberts Papers 3578–3598. Roberts tries her hardest to reassure her future husband in these increasingly affectionate letters.
26 E. Prosser Rhys, Letter to Kate Roberts, 21 November 1928, Kate Roberts Papers NLW KR1 (A) 125.
27 See Nia Williams, '"Fy iaith, fy ngwlad, fy nghenedl": Hanes ymgyrch-oedd gwleidyddol Kate Roberts 1915–1961' (MA thesis, University of Wales, Aberystwyth, 1998). Williams refers to a notebook among Kate Roberts's papers (2559), which mentions Dr William Johnson of Liverpool, a gynaecologist.
28 Morris T. Williams, unposted letter dated 27 August 1927 to E. Prosser Rhys, sealed when received by NLW, Kate Roberts Papers 4213. There are 274 letters from Prosser Rhys to Morris T. Williams in the Kate Roberts Papers in the NLW, dated between 1922 and 1944 (see items 3299–3572).
29 Kate Roberts, 'Byw yn Rhiwbeina', first published in Y Dinesydd (The Citizen), 9 (February/March 1974), reprinted in Erthyglau ac Ysgrifau Llenyddol Kate Roberts, ed. David Jenkins (Swansea: Christopher Davies, 1978), p. 43.

3

1 Kate Roberts, 'Rhigolau Bywyd', in Rhigolau Bywyd a Storïau Eraill (Aberystwyth: Gwasg Aberystwyth, 1929), p. 6.
2 Kate Roberts, 'Y Golled', in Rhigolau Bywyd a Storïau Eraill (Aberystwyth: Gwasg Aberystwyth, 1929), p. 17.
3 Kate Roberts, 'Rhwng dau damaid o gyfleth', in Rhigolau Bywyd a Storïau Eraill (Aberystwyth: Gwasg Aberystwyth, 1929), p. 22.
4 Kate Roberts, 'Nadolig', in Rhigolau Bywyd a Storïau Eraill (Aberystwyth: Gwasg Aberystwyth, 1929), p. 31.
5 Ibid.
6 Kate Roberts, radio interview of 1947, cited in Helen Ungoed Adler, 'Y stori fer Gymraeg 1913–1937' (MA, University of Wales, 1983), 20–1.
7 Derec Llwyd Morgan, Kate Roberts (Cardiff: University of Wales Press, 1991), p. 37.
8 Kate Roberts, 'Y Gwynt', in Rhigolau Bywyd a Storïau Eraill (Aberystwyth: Gwasg Aberystwyth, 1929), p. 47.

[9] D. J. Williams, Letter to Kate Roberts, dated 24 December 1929, NLW Kate Roberts Papers 156.

[10] Francesca Rhydderch, 'Cultural translations: a comparative critical study of Kate Roberts and Virginia Woolf' (Ph.D. thesis, University of Wales, Aberystwyth, 2001), 104.

[11] D. J. Williams, Letter to Kate Roberts, 18 January 1931, NLW Kate Roberts Papers 172.

[12] Kate Roberts, 'Cofio'r dyddiau cynnar yn y Rhondda', *Y Ddraig Goch*, May 1967, reprinted in *Erthyglau ac Ysgrifau Llenyddol Kate Roberts*, ed. David Jenkins (Swansea: Christopher Davies, 1978), pp. 43–5.

[13] Vera Brittain, Letter to Kate Roberts (Mrs Morris Williams), dated 29 November 1933, NLW Kate Roberts Papers 201.

[14] Kate Roberts, 'Dianc', *Y Traethodydd*, 3, 4 (1935), 94–7.

[15] Nia Williams, '"Fy iaith, fy ngwlad, fy nghenedl": hanes ymgyrch-oedd gwleidyddol Kate Roberts 1915–1961' (MA thesis, University of Wales, Aberystwyth, 1998), 64.

[16] Gerwyn Wiliams, *Tir Neb: Rhyddiaith Gymraeg a'r Rhyfel Byd Cyntaf* (Cardiff: University of Wales Press, 1996), p. 142.

[17] Fran Rhydderch notes in this context that the critical neglect of *Tegwch y Bore* may be ascribed to the fact that it is a romance; see Rhydderch, 'Cultural translations', 142.

[18] Allen Raine was the pseudonym of Ada Puddicombe, née Evans, from Ceredigion, who enjoyed immense popular success with novels such as *A Welsh Witch*, *Queen of the Rushes*, *Garthowen*, *A Welsh Singer*, *Torn Sails* and so on, all of which were set in west Wales, published in London, and sold in hundreds of thousands at the turn of the century.

[19] Grace Wynne Griffith, *Creigiau Milgwyn* (Y Bala: Gwasg y Bala, 1935), p. 116.

[20] Kate Roberts, *Traed mewn Cyffion* (1936; Aberystwyth: Gwasg Aber-ystwyth, 1971), pp. 7–8. My translation.

[21] Fran Rhydderch, 'Cultural translations', 152.

[22] Kate Roberts, *Traed mewn Cyffion*, p. 123. Literally, 'to lick the chains of their enslavement'.

[23] Ibid., pp. 138–9.

[24] Kate Roberts, 'Y Garreg Ateb' (1926), NLW Kate Roberts Papers 2861, quoted in Nia Williams, '"Fy iaith, fy ngwlad, fy nghenedl"', 4.

[25] Kate Roberts, *Traed mewn Cyffion*, p. 163.

[26] Ibid., pp. 172–4.

[27] Ibid., pp. 186–7.

[28] Ibid., p.191.

[29] Saunders Lewis, Letter to Kate Roberts, 6 May 1936, NLW Kate Roberts Papers 228; reproduced in *Annwyl Kate, Annwyl Saunders: Gohebiaeth*

1923–1983, ed. Dafydd Ifans (Aberystwyth: Llyfrgell Genedlaethol Cymru, 1992), pp. 114–15.

30 Emyr Humphreys, Review of *Feet in Chains*, trans. by Idwal Walters and John Idris Jones, *Barn*, 179 (December 1977), 414–15.

31 Kate Roberts, 'Buddugoliaeth Alaw Jim', *Ffair Gaeaf* (1937; Denbigh: Gwasg Gee, 1981), p. 9.

32 Raymond Williams, 'The Welsh industrial novel', in Daniel Williams (ed.), *Who Speaks for Wales? Nation, Culture, Identity* (1979; Cardiff: University of Wales Press, 2003), pp. 93–111.

33 Kate Roberts, 'Gorymdaith', *Ffair Gaeaf* (1937; Denbigh: Gwasg Gee, 1981), p. 81.

34 Kate Roberts, 'Dwy Storm', *Ffair Gaeaf* (1937; Denbigh: Gwasg Gee, 1981), p. 44.

35 Kate Roberts, 'Y Taliad Olaf', *Ffair Gaeaf* (1937; Denbigh: Gwasg Gee, 1981), p. 36.

36 Kate Roberts, Interview with Gwyn Erfyl in *Kate Roberts: Ei Meddwl a'i Gwaith*, ed. Rhydwen Williams (Llandybïe: Christopher Davies, 1983), p. 32.

37 Kate Roberts, 'Y Condemniedig', *Ffair Gaeaf* (1937; Denbigh: Gwasg Gee, 1981), p. 72.

38 Kate Roberts, 'Cylch y merched', *Y Ddraig Goch*, 1, 4 (September 1926), 6.

39 Kate Roberts, 'Hen ddodrefn Cymreig', *Y Ddraig Goch*, 1, 6 (November 1926), 6. Note here that the word Roberts uses is 'Cymreig', not 'Cymraeg', meaning Welsh in a wider, cultural sense, not simply the Welsh language.

40 Kate Roberts, 'Chwaneg am addysg merched', *Y Ddraig Goch*, 1, 12 (May 1927), 6.

41 Kate Roberts, 'Pensaerniaeth fel galwedigaeth i ferched', *Y Ddraig Goch*, 2, 1 (June 1927), 6.

42 Nia Williams, '"Fy iaith, fy ngwlad, fy nghenedl"', 59.

43 Kate Roberts, 'Basar fawr y Blaid', *Y Ddraig Goch*, 3, 3 (August 1928), 6.

44 Kate Roberts, 'Ysgol haf Machynlleth 1976', *Y Ddraig Goch*, 4, 2 (July 1929), 6.

45 Kate Roberts, 'Hyn a'r llall' (This and that), *Y Ddraig Goch*, 2, 3 (August 1927), 6.

46 Kate Roberts, 'Arian yw duw Cymru', *Baner ac Amserau Cymru*, 30 June 1948, 8.

47 Kate Roberts, 'Y ferch fodern', *Baner ac Amserau Cymru*, 30 June 1948, 7.

48 Kate Roberts, 'Merched mewn swyddi uchel', *Baner ac Amserau Cymru*, 12 December 1956, 5.

49   Ibid.
50   Fran Rhydderch, '"They do not breed de Beauvoirs here": Kate Roberts's early political journalism', *Yearbook of Welsh Writing in English*, 6 (2000), pp. 21–44 (p. 35).
51   Virginia Woolf, 'Professions for women', *The Death of the Moth and Other Essays* (London: Hogarth Press, 1942).
52   See Jane Aaron, *Nineteenth-century Women's Writing in Wales: Nation, Gender and Identity* (Cardiff: University of Wales Press, 2007); Ceridwen Lloyd-Morgan, 'From temperance to suffrage?', in Angela John (ed.), *Our Mothers' Land: Chapters in Welsh Women's History, 1830–1939* (Cardiff: University of Wales Press, 1991), pp. 135–58.
53   Fran Rhydderch, 'They do not breed de Beauvoirs here', p. 38.

4

1   There are 322 letters of condolence written to Kate Roberts at this time in the Kate Roberts Papers in the NLW 377–69 6 January–11 February 1946. However despairing Roberts felt, at least she could not have thought herself forgotten by friends, relatives and acquaintances.
2   Kate Roberts, Interview with Lewis Valentine, 'Rhwng dau', *Seren Gomer*, 55, 4 (1963), reprinted in *Erthyglau ac Ysgrifau Llenyddol Kate Roberts*, ed. David Jenkins (Swansea: Christopher Davies, 1978), pp. 122–9 (p. 123).
3   Kate Roberts, Journal entry, 3 January 1982, NLW Kate Roberts Papers 2 (A) 2534.
4   Cited in Eigra Lewis Roberts, *Kate Roberts: Llên y Llenor* (Caernarfon: Gwasg Pantycelyn, 1994), p. 96.
5   Saunders Lewis, Letter to Kate Roberts, 27 April 1949, NLW Kate Roberts Papers 804; reproduced in *Annwyl Kate, Annwyl Saunders: Gohebiaeth 1923–1983*, ed. Dafydd Ifans (Aberystwyth: Llyfrgell Genedlaethol Cymru, 1992), p. 149.
6   Aneirin Talfan Davies, Letter to Kate Roberts, Sunday, May/June? 1949, NLW Kate Roberts Papers 811.
7   Kate Roberts, *Stryd y Glep* (Denbigh: Gwasg Gee, 1949), p. 7.
8   Ibid., p. 29.
9   Ibid., p. 94.
10   Kate Roberts, Letter to Saunders Lewis, 12 January 1931, NLW Kate Roberts and Saunders Lewis correspondence 22723D, ff. 74–81; reproduced in *Annwyl Kate, Annwyl Saunders*, p. 72.
11   Storm Jameson, Introduction, *A Summer Day and Other Stories* (Cardiff: Penmark Press, 1946).

12 Copy of *A Summer Day and Other Stories* in the Beinecke Rare Books Library at Yale University is the one that belonged to the poet H. D. (autographed), Za D721 Zz946R. See also H. D. Papers in the Beinecke Library.

13 Storm Jameson, Introduction, p. 7.

14 Ibid., p. 8.

15 Ibid., p. 10.

16 Ibid., p. 14.

17 Kate Roberts, *Modryb a Nith*, NLW Kate Roberts papers 2640–4.

18 Kate Roberts, 'Cwsmeriaid', *Yr Wylan Deg* (1976; Denbigh: Gwasg Gee, 1983), p. 16.

19 Kate Roberts, *Y Byw Sy'n Cysgu* (Dinbych: Gwasg Gee, 1956) p. 82.

20 Ibid., p. 96.

21 Saunders Lewis, Letter to Kate Roberts, Christmas Day 1967, NLW Kate Roberts Papers 1561; reproduced in *Annwyl Kate, Annwyl Saunders*, p. 223. Emphasis in original.

22 Kate Roberts, *Tegwch y Bore* (1967; Llandybïe: Christopher Davies, 1973), p. 142.

23 Ibid., pp. 122–3.

24 Ibid., p. 200.

25 Kate Roberts, Letter to Saunders Lewis, 24 March 1958, NLW Kate Roberts and Saunders Lewis correspondence, 23723 ff. 142–3; reproduced in *Annwyl Kate, Annwyl Saunders*, p. 184.

26 'D. T.', Review of *Te yn y Grug* in *Y Genhinen*, 9, 3 (summer 1959), 189–90.

27 Kate Roberts, 'Te yn y Grug', in *Te yn y Grug* (1959; Dinbych: Gwasg Gee, 1987), p. 41.

28 Ibid.

29 Ibid., p. 42.

30 Ibid., p. 43.

31 Ibid., p. 44.

32 Kate Roberts, 'Dieithrio', in *Te yn y Grug* (1959; Dinbych: Gwasg Gee, 1987), p. 77.

33 Kate Roberts, cited by Ieuan Bryn in *Y Cymro*, August 1973, 16.

34 Kate Roberts, *Y Lôn Wen* (Dinbych: Gwasg Gee, 1960), pp. 10–11.

35 Ibid., p. 20.

36 Ibid., p. 30.

37 Ibid., pp. 152–3.

5

1   Islwyn Ffowc Elis, Review of *Tywyll Heno* in *Lleufer* (winter 1962).

2   Kate Roberts, *Tywyll Heno* (Denbigh: Gwasg Gee, 1962), p. 91.

3   Ibid., pp. 68–9.

4   W. B. Yeats, 'Under Ben Bulben', *Yeats's Poetry, Drama and Prose*, ed. James Pethica (1939; New York: W. W. Norton, 2000), pp. 122–5 (p. 125); Saunders Lewis, 'Queen of Welsh writers', Review of *Hyn o Fyd*, *Western Mail*, 1964.

5   W. B. Yeats, 'Sailing to Byzantium', *Yeats's Poetry, Drama and Prose*, ed. James Pethica (1939; New York: W. W. Norton, 2000) (1928), pp. 80–1 (p. 80).

6   W. B. Yeats, 'Among School Children', *Yeats's Poetry, Drama and Prose*, ed. James Pethica (1939; New York: W. W. Norton, 2000) (1928), pp. 97–8 (p. 97).

7   Correspondence with Lilla Wagner, 1946–1968, NLW Kate Roberts Papers, 714 ff.

8   Kate Roberts, 'Cathod mewn Ocsiwn', *Hyn o Fyd* (Denbigh: Gwasg Gee, 1964), p. 65.

9   Ibid., p. 74.

10 Kate Roberts, Letter to Saunders Lewis, 22 April 1968, NLW Kate Roberts and Saunders Lewis correspondence 22723D ff. 185–6; reproduced in *Annwyl Kate, Annwyl Saunders*, p. 224.

11 Kate Roberts, 'Prynu Dol', *Prynu Dol a Storïau Eraill* (1969; Denbigh: Gwasg Gee, 1981), p. 29.

12 Kate Roberts, 'Blodau', *Prynu Dol a Storïau Eraill* (1969; Denbigh: Gwasg Gee, 1981), p. 61.

13 Ibid.

14 Kate Roberts, 'Gobaith', *Gobaith a Storïau Eraill* (1972; Denbigh: Gwasg Gee, 1982), p. 80.

15 Ibid., p. 86.

16 Kate Roberts, 'Hen Bobl yn Caru', *Yr Wylan Deg a Storïau Eraill* (1976; Denbigh: Gwasg Gee, 1983), p. 42.

17 Aneirin Talfan Davies, Letter to Kate Roberts, November 1976, NLW KR 1877.

18 Kate Roberts, Rhagair, *Haul a Drycin a Storïau Eraill* (Denbigh: Gwasg Gee, 1981), p. 7.

19 Kate Roberts, 'Gwacter', *Haul a Drycin a Storïau Eraill* (Denbigh: Gwasg Gee, 1981), p. 36.

20 Kate Roberts, 'Pryder Morwyn', *Haul a Drycin a Storïau Eraill* (Denbigh: Gwasg Gee, 1981), p. 13.

21 Jean Rhys, cited in Elaine Savory, *Jean Rhys* (Cambridge: Cambridge University Press, 1998), p. 243.

Bibliography

Primary Texts by Kate Roberts

Prose

O Gors y Bryniau (Wrexham: Hughes a'i Fab, 1925).
Deian a Loli (Cardiff: William Lewis, 1927).
Rhigolau Bywyd a Storïau Eraill (Aberystwyth: Gwasg Aberystwyth, 1929).
Laura Jones (Aberystwyth: Gwasg Aberystwyth, 1930).
Traed Mewn Cyffion (Aberystwyth: Gwasg Aberystwyth, 1936).
Ffair Gaeaf a Storïau Eraill (Denbigh: Gwasg Gee, 1937).
Stryd y Glep (Denbigh: Gwasg Gee, 1949).
Y Byw Sy'n Cysgu (Denbigh: Gwasg Gee, 1956).
Te yn y Grug (Denbigh: Gwasg Gee, 1959).
Y Lôn Wen (Denbigh: Gwasg Gee, 1960).
Tywyll Heno (Denbigh: Gwasg Gee, 1962).
Hyn o Fyd (Denbigh: Gwasg Gee, 1963).
Tegwch y Bore (Llandybïe: Llyfrau'r Dryw, 1967) (originally published in instalments in *Y Faner*, 1957–8).
Prynu Dol a Storïau Eraill (Denbigh: Gwasg Gee, 1969).
Gobaith a Storïau Eraill (Denbigh: Gwasg Gee, 1972).
Atgofion, vol. 1 (Porthmadog: Tŷ ar y Graig, 1972), pp. 7–36.
Yr Wylan Deg a Storïau Eraill (Denbigh: Gwasg Gee, 1976).
Erthyglau ac Ysgrifau Llenyddol Kate Roberts, ed. David Jenkins (Swansea: Christopher Davies, 1978)
Haul a Drycin a Storïau Eraill (Denbigh: Gwasg Gee, 1981).

Plays

Co-author with Betty Eynon Davies, *Y Fam* (London and Cardiff: The Educational Publishing Co., 1920).
Co-author with Betty Eynon Davies and Margaret Price, *Y Canpunt: Comedi o Gwm Tawe* (Newtown: The Welsh Outlook Press, 1923).

Co-author with Betty Eynon Davies and Margaret Price, *Wel! Wel! Comedi* (Newtown: The Welsh Outlook Press, 1926).

Ffarwel i Addysg: Comedi mewn Tair Act, unpublished manuscript, 1931; NLW Kate Roberts papers 2515, 2516, 2517.

Y Cynddrws, radio drama, unpublished manuscript; NLW Kate Roberts papers 2637.

Y Gwas, radio drama, unpublished manuscript, 1960–1; NLW Kate Roberts papers 2652.

Modryb a Nith, radio drama, unpublished manuscript, 1959, NLW Kate Roberts papers 2640–4.

Archival sources at the National Library of Wales (NLW)

Kate Roberts Papers 1898–1985, GB 0210 KATERTS, National Library of Wales, 33 boxes of material.

Selected Secondary Texts

Adler, Helen Ungoed, 'Y stori fer Gymraeg 1913–1937' (MA, University of Wales, 1983).

Bowen, Geraint, *Y Traddodiad Rhyddiaith yn yr Ugeinfed Ganrif* (Llandysul: Gomer, 1978).

Brown, Tony, '"Stories from foreign countries": the short stories of Kate Roberts and Margiad Evans', in Alyce von Rothkirch and Daniel Williams (eds), *Beyond the Difference: Welsh Literature in Comparative Contexts*, (Cardiff: University of Wales Press, 2004).

Emyr, John, *Enaid Clwyfus: Golwg ar Waith Kate Roberts* (Dinbych: Gwasg Gee, 1976).

George, Delyth, 'Kate Roberts – ffeminist?', *Y Traethodydd*, 140 (1985), 185–201.

——, 'Llais benywaidd y nofel Gymraeg gyfoes', *Llên Cymru*, XVI (January–July 1991), 363–82.

Gramich, Katie, 'The madwoman in the harness loft: women and madness in the literatures of Wales', in Katie Gramich and Andrew Hiscock (eds), *Dangerous Diversities: The Changing Faces of Wales* (Cardiff: University of Wales Press, 1998).

——, *Twentieth-century Women's Writing in Wales: Land, Gender, Belonging* (Cardiff: University of Wales Press, 2007).

Griffith, Grace Wynne, *Creigiau Milgwyn* (Y Bala: Gwasg y Bala, 1935).

Harris, John, 'A long low sigh across the waters: the first translations of Kate Roberts', *Planet*, 87 (June/July, 1991), 20–9.

Humphreys, Emyr, *The Triple Net: a Portrait of the Writer Kate Roberts, 1891–1985* (London: Channel 4 Television, 1988).

Ifans, Dafydd, ed., *Annwyl Kate, Annwyl Saunders: Gohebiaeth 1923–1983* (Aberystwyth: Llyfrgell Genedlaethol Cymru, 1992).

Jarvis, Branwen, 'Kate Roberts and a woman's world', *Transactions of the Honourable Society of Cymmrodorion* (1991), 233–48.

Jones, Bobi (ed.), *Kate Roberts: Cyfrol Deyrnged* (Dinbych: Gwasg Gee, 1969).

Jones, Harri Pritchard, ed., Rhagymadrodd, *Goreuon Storïau Kate Roberts* (Dinbych: Gwasg Gee, 1997).

Jones, John Gwilym, *Crefft y Llenor* (Denbigh; Gwasg Gee, 1977).

——, 'Y llenor cydwladol Cymreig', *Y Casglwr*, 26 (August 1985), 6.

Jones, R. Gerallt, 'An introduction to the work of Kate Roberts', *Anglo-Welsh Review*, 9, 24 (1958), 10–21.

Knight, Stephen, '"The hesitations and uncertainties that were the truth": three women writers of Welsh industrial fiction', in H. Gustav Klaus and Stephen Knight (eds), *British Industrial Fictions* (Cardiff: University of Wales Press, 2000).

Lewis, Saunders, Interview with Kate Roberts in *Crefft y Stori Fer* (Llandysul: Y Clwb Llyfrau Cymreig, 1949).

Lloyd, D. Myrddin, 'Kate Roberts', Aneurin Talfan Davies (ed.), *Gŵyr Llên* [*sic*] (Aberystwyth: W. Griffiths and Sons, 1948), pp. 213–28.

Llwyd, Alan and Elwyn Edwards, Y *Bardd a Gollwyd* (Swansea: Barddas, 1992).

Miles, M. H., 'Y stori fer yng Nghymru' (MA thesis, University of Wales, Bangor, 1979).

Morgan, Derec Llwyd, *Bro a Bywyd Kate Roberts* (Caerdydd: Cyngor Celfyddydau Cymru, 1981).

——, *Kate Roberts* (Cardiff: University of Wales Press, 1991). First published in 1974 in the Writers of Wales series.

Morgan, Mihangel, 'Kate yn y Cwm', in Hywel Teifi Edwards (ed.), *Cwm Cynon* (Llandysul: Gomer, 1997), pp. 285–308.

Morris, Phoebe Hopkin, 'Atgofion am Dr Kate Roberts', *Y Gwyliedydd*, 30 May 1985.

Rhydderch, Francesca, 'Cultural translations: a comparative critical study of Kate Roberts and Virginia Woolf' (Ph.D. thesis, University of Wales, Aberystwyth, 2001).

——, '"They do not breed de Beauvoirs here": Kate Roberts's early political journalism', *Yearbook of Welsh Writing in English*, 6 (2006), pp. 21–44.

——, 'Cyrff yn cyffwrdd: darlleniadau erotig o Kate Roberts', *Taliesin*, 99 (1997), 86–97.

Roberts, Eigra Lewis, *Kate Roberts: Llên y Llenor* (Caernarfon: Gwasg Pantycelyn, 1994).

Roberts, J., 'Astudiaeth o waith diweddar Kate Roberts' (MA thesis, University of Wales, Aberystwyth, 1975).

Rowlands, John, *Ysgrifau ar y Nofel* (Cardiff: University of Wales Press, 1992).

Thomas, M. Wynn, *DiFfinio Dwy Lenyddiaeth Cymru* (Cardiff: University of Wales Press, 1995).

Thomas, Ned, *The Welsh Extremist* (London: Gollancz, 1971), chapter 6.

Tomos, Dewi, *Llyfr Lloffion Cae'r Gors* (Llanrwst: Gwasg Carreg Gwalch, 2009).

Williams, Gerwyn, *Tir Neb: Rhyddiaith Gymraeg a'r Rhyfel Byd Cyntaf* (Cardiff: University of Wales Press, 1996).

—— (ed.), *Rhyddid y Nofel* (Cardiff: University of Wales Press, 1999).

Williams, Herbert, 'Kate Roberts in person'(interview), *Planet*, 42 (April 1978), 26–30.

Williams, Jeni, 'The place of fantasy: children and narratives in two short stories by Kate Roberts and Dylan Thomas', *Yearbook of Welsh Writing in English*, 6, pp. 46–66.

Williams, J. E. Caerwyn, Interview with Kate Roberts, *Ysgrifau Beirniadol*, III (Denbigh, 1967).

Williams, Nia, '"Fy iaith, fy ngwlad, fy nghenedl": hanes ymgyrchoedd gwleidyddol Kate Roberts 1915–1961' (unpublished MA thesis, University of Wales Aberystwyth, 1998).

Williams, Rhydwen (ed.), *Kate Roberts: ei Meddwl a'i Gwaith* (Llandybïe: Christopher Davies, 1983).

Selected Translations

'The Victory of Alaw Jim', trans. Walter Dowding, *Life and Letters Today 'Welsh Number'*, 24, 31 (March 1940), 280–7.

A Summer Day and Other Stories (Cardiff: Penmark Press, 1946) (Introduction by Storm Jameson).

Tea in the Heather, trans. Wyn Griffith (Ruthin: John Jones, 1968).

'Cats at an Auction', trans. Wyn Griffith, in Gwyn Jones and Islwyn Ffowc Elis (eds), *Twenty-five Welsh Short Stories* (London: Oxford University Press, 1971).

The Living Sleep, trans. Wyn Griffith (Cardiff: John Jones, 1976).

Feet in Chains, trans. Idwal Walters and John Idris Jones (Cardiff: John Jones, 1977).

Two Old Men & Other Stories, trans. Wyn Griffith and Elan Closs Stephens, illustrated by Kyffin Williams (Tregynon: Gwasg Gregynog, 1981).

The World of Kate Roberts: Selected Stories 1925–1981, ed. Joseph P. Clancy (Philadelphia: Temple University Press, 1991).

Sun and Storm and Other Stories, trans. Carolyn Watcyn (Denbigh: Gwasg Gee, 2000).

The Awakening, trans. Siân James (Bridgend: Seren, 2006).

One Bright Morning, trans. Gillian Clarke (Llandysul: Gomer, 2008).

The White Lane, trans. Gillian Clarke (Llandysul: Gomer, 2009).

Kate Roberts: Tee drinken op de heide, trans. Vertaald door Dries Janssen (Antwerpen: Etnika, 1969).

Treid daouhualet, trans. J. Abasq (Brest: Brud nevez, 1988).

La mouette et autres nouvelles galloises, trans. Jean Hamard (Paris: Les Belles Lettres, 1993).

Katzen auf einer Versteigerung, trans. Wolfgang Schamoni (Bielefeld: Pendragon, 2000).

Index